Legal WRITING

How to Write Legal Briefs, Memos, and Other Legal Documents in a Clear and Concise Style

AMANDA MARTINSEK

PUBLISHING

New York

For my boys, Jack, Thomas, and Paul.
They really aren't certain what I do
and have no idea why it takes so long!

* * *

Published by Kaplan Publishing, a division of Kaplan, Inc.
1 Liberty Plaza, 24th Floor
New York, NY 10006

Printed in the United States of America

Library of Congress Cataloging-in-Publication Data

Martinsek, Amanda.
Legal writing: how to write legal briefs, memos, and other legal documents in a clear and concise style/Amanda Martinsek.
p. cm.
Includes index.
1. Legal composition. I. Title.
KF250.M372 2009
808'.06634—dc22

2008040368

10 9 8 7 6 5 4 3 2 1
ISBN-13: 978-1-4277-9843-5

Contents

Preface

FILMS AND TELEVISION SHOWS LEAVE the impression that the life of a lawyer is spent largely in the courtroom, that even the most complex cases may be resolved through oral argument alone, and that lawyers rarely if ever have cause to set pen to paper. However, despite the prominent role legal oratory plays in the popular media, most courtroom battles are fought, won, and lost on paper. Writing a coherent, persuasive legal argument is an advocate's most powerful weapon. Even so, lawyers throughout the world are constantly searching for precisely the right words to define transactions and relationships of all kinds. Whether a trial or a transactional lawyer, the most successful attorney is one who focuses on developing writing skills as a necessary complement to knowledge of the law.

The public's image of legal writing is one of incomprehensible Latin phrases interspersed with "whereases," "heretofores," and "hereunders." Effective legal writing could not be more different. Today the goal is to use as few words as possible to present arguments clearly and forcefully. This book will demonstrate how to make your writing work for you in today's evolving legal environment—because although acceptable writing can make a good lawyer, good writing can make a great lawyer.

The quality of legal writing can literally change a client's destiny. The words that a lawyer selects and the arguments that a lawyer crafts can make the difference between freedom and incarceration, between success and bankruptcy. A compelling argument may get lost in arcane syntax and poor organization—sometimes even when used by an experienced attorney. A critical contract point can be left ambiguous and uncertain, producing an unintended result as the relationships of the parties evolve over time. In this book, you will be given the tools to distinguish good writing from bad, and you will become familiar with the rules you need to follow to effectively represent your clients in the courtroom or the boardroom.

Good legal writing involves more than grammar and punctuation. The first section of this book gives an overview of the role of writing in our legal system. You will learn about the essential documents of civil and criminal proceedings, and you will read about drafting transactional documents. This section also emphasizes the vital role that research and interpretation play in oral and written advocacy.

The second section focuses on how to use the principles of good English to make your own writing clear and persuasive. You will be shown how to organize your thoughts, present your message, and style your documents in ways that will engage your clients, judges, and opposing counsel and speak to them with equal force and clarity.

The third section focuses on the application of strong writing skills to create legal documents that will serve your clients in and out of court. The distinctions between memoranda, pleadings, discovery requests, briefs, and other filings will be discussed, as well as strategies to make each kind of document as effective as possible. Various types of letters that you will encounter in practice will be reviewed, and you will learn how to effectively represent yourself and your clients in your office, in the field, and before the bench.

Legal writing has long been a source of derision and bad jokes. Lawyers who can write documents that are immediately accessible to both clients and judges, however, command respect and influence decisions.

Instead of cutting and pasting language from old briefs and agreements, skillful legal writers produce well-edited, streamlined communications that are reshaping the way people think about legal writing. When courts impose page limits, lawyers who have learned how to write well are a step ahead, able to focus on arguing a case succinctly instead of trying to fudge the margins.

Good writing enhances the attorney's courtroom performance as well as building a reputation. Information presented clearly can help a legal firm in its offices as much as in the courtroom. Lawyers who are accessible to clients begin winning their cases before even approaching the bench. Every memorandum, every table and chart, every paragraph of every motion is focused on the facts at hand, with no obfuscation or indecision. Clear writing in an approachable style ensures effective communication, and effective communication is the first step to success. Whether you are writing a contract, filing a brief, or just gaining a better sense of legal practices, this book will help you get started.

Part I

Overview

Chapter 1

Introduction to the Legal System

AS YOU BEGIN LEGAL WRITING, bear in mind the framework that surrounds and guides your actions every day: the American legal system. A legal system functions to hold a government together and, in a reciprocal manner, the government works to keep that system running. There are three main types of laws that underlie the legal systems of the world: civil law, religious law, and common law. Civil law, or European continental law, dominates European systems but is not exclusive to that region. Civil law has its basis in legislation, a concept we will explore later in this chapter. Religious law exists in states of government that rely on religious documents as legal doctrine or a theological system as a source of legal reasoning. Common law, although it certainly can and has been influenced by both civil and religious laws, represents a constantly evolving legal system. Common law is a framework which evolves through court decisions. The American legal system operates with common law as its template but does not amount to a pure common law system. Instead, American jurisprudence amalgamates common and civil law with federalism. A federal legal system is marked by its negotiation of power between the central authority and individuals. The federal body of law constitutes a well-oiled, albeit complicated, machine that combines common law with administrative, statutory, and, perhaps most conspicuously, constitutional law. Before we begin to explore the interaction of these laws, let's examine the history of the United States legal system.

IN THIS CHAPTER	
• **History of the U.S. Legal System** ◦ Why Is the American Legal System So Effective? ◦ Benefits • **Jurisdiction**	• **Sources of Substantive Law** ◦ State and Federal Government • **Major Areas of U.S. Legal System** ◦ Civil ◦ Criminal • **Summation**

HISTORY OF THE U.S. LEGAL SYSTEM

The American government as we know it has its roots in the legal traditions of Great Britain. The United States was created both in opposition to and in tribute to the British system of government. Although many people are quick to point out the differences between the governments of the two nations, the similarities are equally striking. Among other things, common law, or "law of procedure," yokes the two countries. Common law relies on customs and judicial recognition of those customs. The United States used common law practices to guide court decisions and to define the judicial branch of its government. The U.S. system of government also modeled many aspects of its legislative branch on the British Parliament. The most obvious difference—and the primary source of contention—between the British and the American forms of government is the monarchy. America's determination to break from the Crown is what originally defined this nation and established its direction along a more egalitarian course. Although America did not want a king or queen, it needed a leader, someone who could both literally and symbolically hold the country together. The executive branch was created in recognition that although the country would not tolerate a king, it did want a person in power: the president.

Why Is the American Legal System So Effective?

Although choosing the "best" form of government relies to some degree on value-laden assumptions, it is fair to say that the American system has been effective as evidenced by both its longevity and its economic success. But why has it been so effective? There are two reasons: predictability and enforceability.

- **Predictability.** Did you ever have a teacher who gave you a new set of rules every week? Have you ever bent the rules for your son and then been slammed by your daughter for unfair parenting? Chances are the consequences of these deviations were minor (since they involved only yourself and a few others). Imagine if the rules, or laws, of your country changed periodically. Confusion and resentment understandably result when a country applies its laws inconsistently. Whatever criticisms one might have of the American legal system, by and large, it is predictable.
- **Enforceability.** Once people have been given an opportunity to become familiar with the laws, those laws are much easier to enforce. In fact, as long as laws are seen as predictable by the people, the government can enforce them without worrying about confusion. But there are a lot of people in this country and so many laws to oversee. Who is responsible for enforcing what? Who speaks for the law? Who has jurisdiction?

JURISDICTION

To understand who enforces the laws and who must obey the laws, we turn to the 1787 Constitutional Convention. One of the main questions the U.S. delegates focused on during their meetings was where ultimate authority would rest. Many of the delegates wanted the states to retain the majority of the power. Today, the idea of each state having ultimate power might sound extreme but, at the time of the Convention, many of the most powerful and influential delegates were federalists. Giving controlling power to the central government was controversial due to the sheer size of America. Past republics had been successful only within small countries and in 1787, historically, had almost always given rise to the dominance of a tyrannical leader.

Despite the initial disagreements, ultimately the federalists pushed through their platform for a central federal government that would retain jurisdiction over the states. The states, in turn, were given power over their own citizens. The reach of federal jurisdiction extends all over the United States whereas a state's jurisdiction ends at its boundaries. For instance, there was a time when an 18-year-old could buy alcohol in the state of Wisconsin. Many young citizens of Illinois (where the drinking age was 21) traveled north to the Dairy State in those days. Even though it was illegal in most states for them to drink alcohol, if they were in Wisconsin it was perfectly legal. Much to their chagrin, Illinois lawmakers and law enforcers did not (and still do not) have jurisdiction over their citizens' actions in Wisconsin.

Jurisdiction, or the ability to exercise authority, is defined on three levels: subject matter jurisdiction, personal jurisdiction, and jurisdiction within a specific place. Jurisdiction will usually be used here to refer to the court's authority.

- **Subject matter jurisdiction.** This refers to what matters a court can adjudicate.
- **Personal jurisdiction.** This defines the parties the court can force to comply with its orders.
- **Jurisdiction within a certain place.** As mentioned above, a state lacks the jurisdiction to tell those outside its borders how to behave. The federal government, however, has jurisdiction over certain specified matters in each and every state.

SOURCES OF SUBSTANTIVE LAW

Now that we know who has authority to enforce the laws, we need to understand what types of laws are being enforced. Substantive law refers to the laws that define rights and duties. Within substantive law there is statutory law and common law. We covered common law earlier in this chapter, but to review, common law is the product of decisions made by the courts. Once a court has ruled on a particular matter, that ruling becomes judicial

precedent. That precedent forms the framework that subsequent courts apply to similar fact patterns. In contrast, statutory law is created by the legislative or executive branch. Both types of law govern the actions of American citizens. This should give you at least a preliminary sense of the checks and balances at play among America's three branches of government.

State and Federal Government

One of the defining features of the American legal system is its use of three branches to govern one nation. While the executive, legislative, and judicial branches have their roots (no pun intended) in the British monarchy, Parliament, and courts, respectively, they are distinguished from their British model by their use of checks and balances. Through this system, each branch exercises limits over the powers of the others. The power of the legislative branch is limited by the authority of the executive. If the executive seems to be wielding undue power, the judicial branch will review the acts of the executive and take any necessary corrective actions. Each of the three branches is unique and has its own roles to perform both in terms of its own responsibilities and in relation to the two other branches. It might help to visualize a Venn diagram as you think about the checks and balances among the three branches. The three overlapping branches have areas in common, and thus areas that serve to keep one another in check. At the same time, each branch reserves exclusive rights to compensate and balance the relationship. The principle of checks and balances arises in all areas of legal practice.

The exclusive duties of the three branches of the U.S. government are as follows:

- **Executive branch.** An elected president and his or her chosen cabinet must "take care that the laws are faithfully executed."
- **Legislative branch.** Elected members of Congress, comprised by the House of Representatives and the Senate, write the federal laws.
- **Judicial branch.** Appointed federal judges decide legal cases. As a lawyer, the judicial branch is where you will likely spend the most time. Within the judicial branch, you will try cases. These cases will generally be categorized as either civil or criminal.

MAJOR AREAS OF U.S. LEGAL SYSTEM

There are many areas of legal practice in the United States, but all can ultimately be categorized into two groups: *civil* and *criminal*. Within each category of law there are many specializations; for brevity's sake, we'll go over only a few.

Civil Law

In a civil lawsuit, a party personally initiates and finances a lawsuit against a defendant for money damages to compensate for physical, financial, or emotional harm. The purpose of a civil lawsuit is not punitive but rather to achieve economic redress for someone who has suffered a compensable wrong. For example, if a car crashes into your home, you are permitted to file a lawsuit against the driver to recover the money necessary to repair the damage. Within civil law, the specializations of commercial and corporate law implicate different methods of writing legal documents.

- **Commercial law** enables an individual to enter into enforceable contracts with others. Modern commercial law is generally governed by both the common law and a state enacted statute called the Uniform Commercial Code (UCC). The common law governs transactions in land and services whereas the UCC generally regulates sales of goods between merchants. As an example of a commercial suit, if you made a contract to buy your neighbor's house and your neighbor later refuses to sell it to you because a third party offered him more money, you could sue your neighbor in an effort to enforce the contract.
- **Corporate law** governs the creation and function of corporations. This area of law might involve the actual drafting of the corporate charter, which outlines the corporation's purposes and bylaws. It might also deal with conflicts between stockholders and the board of directors.

Criminal Law

Criminal law differs from civil law in several key aspects. First, a criminal lawsuit is brought by the state against the defendant. Second, the purposes of the lawsuit are different from those of civil law. Whereas a civil lawsuit is filed to obtain monetary remediation for damages or perhaps to enjoin certain behavior, criminal prosecutions are for the purpose of deterring the charged individual and future potential criminals from committing more crimes, as well as punishing the perpetrator. Third, the standard of proof in a criminal prosecution is significantly higher, since the potential consequences for a criminal defendant include incarceration or death. That is not to say, however, that criminal law and civil law do not overlap. For example, if a bar fight breaks out and someone injures another, the aggressor might be charged by the state for assault and battery, as well as be sued in civil court by the injured party to recover damages relating to the injuries.

SUMMATION

We will discuss criminal and civil law in much more detail in the following chapters. Bear in mind that the American legal system continues to function as an effective process because of its common law roots. State and federal laws do not depend solely on legislation to guide the legal process. The relationship among the three U.S. government branches highlights the importance of checks and balances. The judicial branch plays a critical role in interpreting the laws created by as well as the scope of authority vested in the other respective branches.

Chapter 2

Civil Litigation in Brief

AT SOME POINT IN LAW school you will be expected to take a class in civil procedure. Civil procedure lays out the rules that govern the civil side of the American legal system. In essence, civil procedure creates the rules of the game. Sometimes the rules can be tedious to study and remember. But you will find that without these rules you would not even know where to begin your case. Without civil procedure, trying a case would be like playing football without referees, boundaries, a scoreboard, or any other organizational means to keep the "sport" legitimate. The procedural rules follow the same principles as the Constitution and maintain the principle of checks and balances that was discussed in the last chapter. Our court system is designed to produce a fair and factually based judgment for each case brought before it. The Rules of Civil Procedure are the gatekeepers for the various stages of litigation and are designed to enable litigants to gather all relevant facts and to proceed on a level playing field. In this chapter you will learn the basic procedures of civil litigation and the policies behind them. We will cover criminal litigation in another chapter.

IN THIS CHAPTER	
• **Pleading Stage** ○ Complaint ○ Defendant's Responses to Complaint • **Discovery Stage** ○ Purpose of Discovery ○ Types of Discovery ○ Motions to Compel Production	• **Motion for Summary Judgment** • **Trials** ○ Bench Trials ○ Jury Trials • **Intermediate Appeal** • **Court of Last Resort** • **Summation**

PLEADING STAGE

Civil litigation begins in much the same way as an academic paper you might have written as an undergraduate. The pleading stage requires identification of the themes that will drive the overall dispute toward a final judgment. The legitimacy of a plaintiff's claim is what is at stake throughout the pleading stage. This stage involves a series of steps to determine whether a claim is valid, beginning with a complaint.

Complaint

A case begins with the filing of a *complaint.* The complaint may also be known as a *petition.* The one filing the complaint in court is known as the *plaintiff.* The plaintiff can be an individual, a group of people, or an entity such as a corporation. The complaint sets forth allegations against the party known as the *defendant.* The defendant also may be an entity or one or more persons. The plaintiff may assert one or more *causes of action* in the lawsuit. These causes of action are also known as the *claims* or *counts* against the defendant. *Claim, cause of action,* or *count* is a term that refers to a legal theory for a party's liability. Characteristically, there is a *prayer* or *demand* for relief associated with each claim. The demand for relief in civil litigation usually takes the form of monetary compensation, although it can refer to other sorts of relief, such as giving back what was taken or the initiation of or refraining from some action.

Defendant's Responses to Complaint

Once a complaint is filed, the defendant has three possible responses: a motion to dismiss, an answer, or an answer with a counterclaim.

- **Motion to dismiss.** The defendant may file a motion to dismiss plaintiff's complaint. Generally, a motion to dismiss assumes the facts of plaintiff's complaint to be true but argues that no claim exists based on those facts. The brief supporting a motion to dismiss should explain all of the legal reasons dismissal is required. In many ways, a motion to dismiss is like a teacher listing all the weak aspects of a paper you have written. The motion, like that teacher's red pen, highlights the problems with the argument and includes a series of logical or factual errors. The plaintiff, unlike most students meeting with their teachers, is allowed to comment on the defendant's brief and argue why the complaint is sufficient. A judge will then decide who has the stronger argument and whether or not to grant the defendant's motion to dismiss. The case may be dismissed with or without prejudice if the judge grants the motion. A judge may also give a plaintiff leave to amend—an opportunity to fix the problems in the complaint. The plaintiff has the right to appeal to a higher court if the court grants a motion to dismiss.
    - Defendant files a brief explaining its legal reasons.
    - Plaintiff must file a response brief that addresses the defendant's arguments.
    - In some cases defendant files a reply brief reinforcing its arguments.
    - Judge may hear oral arguments as well as reading the briefs.
    - Judge then decides whether to grant the motion. If the motion is granted, the case is dismissed; however, the plaintiff may appeal the case in a higher court.
    - The party making a motion is known as the *movant.*
    - The party opposing the motion is known as the *nonmoving party* or opponent.

- **Answer.** Any defendant that does not make a motion to dismiss must answer the complaint. An answer serves as an acknowledgment that the defendant is aware of the case and gives the defendant an opportunity to choose which of the complaint's allegations to dispute or admit. If the defendant does not answer in time, the plaintiff can ask for default judgment. Once the defendant has answered, the plaintiff cannot file a response or an amended complaint unless the court grants leave. The answer may identify new facts relevant to the matters raised by the complaint, as well as defenses.
- **Answer with a counterclaim.** A third option for the defendant is to answer a complaint and also to state a counterclaim. A counterclaim is a statement of the defendant's own allegations and claims against the plaintiff. The counterclaim must be answered by the plaintiff. An effective counterclaim may counterbalance a complaint. A counterclaim can be either compulsory or permissive.
  - A *compulsory counterclaim* cannot be made during a separate legal proceeding. A counterclaim is determined to be compulsory if it involves the same parties and the same facts and occurrences as the original lawsuit. For instance, if it is alleged that the defendant hit the plaintiff, after which the plaintiff picked up a shovel and conked the defendant on the head, the defendant's counterclaim would be considered compulsory because it occurred in the same setting and time frame and between the same people.
  - A *permissive counterclaim* can be made in conjunction with the current case or at a later time. Unlike a compulsory counterclaim, a permissive counterclaim may involve further complications, a broader time frame and, perhaps, more parties. For instance, the plaintiff was allegedly hit by the defendant one night at a bar. The plaintiff also owes the defendant and his partner for a piece of real estate. The defendant is given

permission by the court system to make the strategic decision between answering the original lawsuit with a counterclaim and initiating a new case.

DISCOVERY STAGE

The discovery stage in the lawsuit is like the research stage of writing a paper. Throughout the discovery stage you will need to do a lot of grunt work while keeping in mind the procedural rules governing how you obtain your facts and requiring that you share what you know with the court and your opposing counsel.

Purpose of Discovery

A lawyer should know all the facts of a case before going to trial. Even though you will learn a lot about the case from your own client, private investigators, and cooperative third parties, you also must obtain information from your opponent and less forthcoming third parties. The acquisition of your opponent's information in a civil matter is known as discovery. The proper procedure for discovery involves a give-and-take between the lawyers. The plaintiff and the defendant each have the right to discovery. If a great deal is at stake, both parties will most likely use all the types of discovery they have at their disposal.

Types of Discovery

There are four types of discovery between parties: requests for admission, requests for production of documents and things, interrogatories, and depositions.

- **Request for admission.** A party submits a factual statement to its opponent. The opposing party must either admit or deny the statement. If a party admits a statement to be true, the admission establishes a fact for trial. There are exceptions to this rule that occur in unique and rare circumstances.
- **Request for production of documents and things.** Each party is allowed to request files, data, and any other

relevant items of interest from the opposing party. This is also known simply as a document request.

- **Interrogatories.** Each party is permitted to write questions to the other that require sworn responses. The plaintiff, for example, might ask the defendant to verify that he was at a movie at a certain time on a certain date. The defendant would then answer each question and end with "I swear that the above responses are true and correct."
- **Depositions.** The final type of discovery allows the parties to depose any witnesses. A witness may be a party to the case, a representative or agent of a party, or a non-party. Depositions are formal proceedings that all parties have the right to attend. The witness is placed under oath. Lawyers representing the parties may question the witness. A court reporter takes down everything that is said during the depositions. Anything the court reporter transcribes becomes a part of the record.

Motions to Compel Production

As wonderful as it would be to be able to trust the opposing party to provide all the information it should, many times this is not the case. Because parties sometimes withhold information, each party has the right to file a motion to compel production of documents or information. For instance, if the plaintiff believes that the defendant is failing to produce a document, the plaintiff can file a motion to compel production. The defendant can then answer the motion by either denying possession of the document or asserting the right not to produce it. The judge will ultimately decide which side makes the better argument and will either grant or deny the motion to compel production.

MOTION FOR SUMMARY JUDGMENT

It is important to bear in mind that civil cases seldom go to trial. This is due, in part, to the alternative of *summary judgment.* A summary judgment motion relies on a background of material facts that are not in dispute. A case's material facts are those that are relevant to the elements (the legal underpinnings) of the claims for relief. A movant, or the party making the motion for summary judgment, will argue that the material facts are not in dispute and, as a legal matter, based on those facts, no jury could find in favor of the non-moving party. This motion will usually occur after the discovery stage since it would be difficult to argue that the material facts are not in dispute if all facts have not yet been ascertained. The non-moving party may file a memorandum in response. A movant may then be permitted a reply brief. As with the other motions discussed, the judge decides between the two opponents' arguments. The judge will either grant summary judgment or the case will move on to trial.

TRIALS

Although comparitively infrequent, the trial is the most publicized stage in the process of a case. Movies and television shows tend to depict lawyers as constantly battling one another in the courtroom. Even though a case may be decided in a party's favor anywhere along the line, the trial carries a certain symbolic weight that a summary judgment or motion to dismiss does not. One reason for this is the public's sense of familiarity with a trial as opposed to the other stages of litigation. Because trials are inherently public proceedings, in addition to their popularity as a dramatic device, people tend to have more basic knowledge about the procedure of a trial than, say, about the procedures of discovery.

There are two types of trial: *bench trial* and *jury trial.* The jury trial is more procedurally complex than the bench trial.

Bench Trials

In a bench trial, the judge decides the issues of both law and fact. Both sides present their cases and the judge weighs the two to reach a final judgment. The bench trial procedure is in keeping with all of the procedures we have gone over earlier in this chapter. As with a motion to dismiss or for summary judgment, a judge evaluates the two arguments and determines their respective strengths and weaknesses based on the validity of their claims and evidence. In those motions, however, the facts are not in dispute and, thus there are no factual determinations to be made. In a bench trial, the judge also decides the facts. Each side is allowed to make an opening statement, present witnesses, and introduce documents and exhibits relevant to the case. Each side is also allowed to cross-examine witnesses produced by the opposing party and is allowed to make closing statements.

Jury Trials

A jury trial involves both the judge and a jury. The jury decides the issues of fact. The judge instructs the jury on the law and applies the rules of evidence to determine what a jury sees and hears. As with the bench trial, both parties are allowed to make opening statements, present witnesses, and introduce documents and exhibits relevant to the case. Each side is also allowed to cross-examine witnesses produced by the opposing party and to make closing statements. When both sides have presented their cases, the judge instructs the jury on the legal issues. The jury will then deliberate and try to reach a verdict.

If a verdict is not reached, a mistrial will be declared and a new trial ordered. If a verdict is reached, the losing party may make a *post-trial motion* arguing that the jury's verdict should not stand. With this motion, as with the motions discussed earlier, the judge is in the driver's seat. Most post-trial motions give the judge three options:

- The judge may deny the motion and enter a final judgment based on the jury's verdict.
- The judge may grant the motion and order a completely new trial with a new jury.
- The judge may grant the motion and award a final judgment notwithstanding the verdict.

INTERMEDIATE APPEAL

After the final judgment at trial, achieved by judicial decision, jury verdict, or post-trial judgment, the losing party still has options. At this point, the losing side is known as the *appellant* or petitioner. Like a petition that begins any case, an *intermediate appeal* must be filed as a claim to a hearing by the higher court. This appeal must brief the court on one or more errors that were made at trial. Like the motions in the earlier stages of the case, the appeal is subject to the standard give-and-take inherent in the court system. Once the appeal is filed, it is up to the responding party, known as the *appellee,* to file its own brief in response to the appellant's appeal. The appellant can then reply to the appellee's brief. The appellate court will then hear oral arguments from both parties, and then it will affirm or reverse the trial court's judgment. The court can affirm or reverse certain parts of the ruling and not others. If the court does reverse the ruling, it can issue its own judgment or order a new trial with new instructions. If a case is reversed, the appellate court will most frequently order a new trial.

COURT OF LAST RESORT

There is still one more stage in the appeal process: *the court of last resort.* The loser at the intermediate appeal level can appeal to this court, which is also the highest court in a jurisdiction. The court of last resort decides whether or not to hear a case. There is no such thing as a "right" to the court of last resort; it's better viewed as a privilege. But if the court does decide to hear the case, the appellate process is repeated, with both sides presenting their cases one last time, through briefs and oral arguments. The court of last resort will then review the intermediate court's ruling and affirm or reverse it. If the ruling is reversed, the court of last resort will either issue its own judgment or remand with instructions—which may include instructions to convene a new trial.

SUMMATION

The legal system, like any social institution, relies on a structured set of rules and conventions in order to function. These rules, collectively known in the civil context as the Rules of Civil Procedure, are the product of centuries of tradition complemented by legislative reforms and newly established precedents. If you want to be a player in the legal system, you will have to play by the rules. The litigation stages and procedures highlighted here can serve as the beginning point to a detailed study of the laws and principles underlying the U.S. court system.

Chapter 3

Criminal Law in Brief

THE LINE THAT DIVIDES CIVIL law and criminal law is largely determined by their contextual differences. This chapter discusses what defines criminal law, the procedures involved in the various stages of criminal law, and the overarching principles that guide the process.

IN THIS CHAPTER	
• **Applicable Statute** ◦ Types of Jurisdiction ◦ Unlawful Action ◦ Determination and Definition of Intent ◦ Punishment • **Pre-Arraignment** ◦ Booking • **Bail**	• **Arraignment** ◦ Trial Procedure ◦ Trial Schedule • **Trial** ◦ Judge or Jury Trial ◦ Trial Steps • **Sentencing** ◦ Alternatives to Sentencing • **Appeals** • **Summation**

APPLICABLE STATUTE

An applicable statute helps us understand what distinguishes criminal law from civil law. As a reminder, a statute is a rule determined by the federal, state, or local government. When you are charged with breaking a statute, you are assumed to be going against the state and are therefore considered a threat to the state. When you are charged in a civil case, you are only accused of going against the rights and liberties of another individual or group.

Types of Jurisdiction

The three basic forms of criminal jurisdiction are federal, state, and local.

- **Federal.** Although most criminal activity is regulated by states, Congress has the ability to regulate activities prohibited by the Constitution, as well as interstate crimes. In recent years, Congress has exercised sweeping powers under the Commerce Clause.
- **State.** The state defines and determines the punishment of a variety of crimes from trespass to homicide.
- **Local.** The local jurisdiction has power over nuisance crimes or ordinance violations.

Unlawful Action

Unlawful action is precisely that: action that is against the law. An unlawful action is any action that is defined as unlawful under an applicable criminal statute. This is one of the distinguishing features between criminal law and civil law. Although you can be sued in civil court any time you cause harm or violate a duty of care, under criminal law you can be prosecuted only if your action is defined as a crime under a statute. For example, suppose a new drug is created that is not forbidden under a statute. A doctor negligently prescribes the drug, which results in the patient's death. Although the patient's family can sue the doctor in civil court for negligence, the state cannot prosecute the doctor for giving the patient the drug because it is not illegal (assuming the doctor has not broken some other statute outlining prescription procedures). If the doctor had given the patient an illegal drug, he could be both sued in civil court and prosecuted by the state. One of the most interesting aspects of criminal law concerns just what makes certain actions worthy of being called "criminal." Although this subject is too complex to discuss in detail here, it generally entails the concepts of retribution, deterrence, incapacitation, and rehabilitation.

Determination and Definition of Intent

Mental State

Traditionally under the common law, there was no crime unless the action, or *actus reus*, was committed under the proper mental state, or *mens rea*. Mens rea can best be described as "culpability." Mens rea is a subjective mental state that makes a defendant's actions sufficiently blameworthy to justify prosecution by the state. Thus, to be guilty of murder, you must not only have killed someone, but you must have done the killing with the proper mental state. The concept of mens rea is linked with the purposes of criminal law, such as the punishment of someone who deserves it. This is why civil law generally is concerned not with the subjective mental state of the defendant, but only with the defendant's objective actions. Although the mens rea requirement captures an important aspect of what makes certain actions criminal, the definition is somewhat murky. The Model Penal Code (MPC) represents an attempt to clarify modes of culpability. Instead of relying on the general concept of mens rea, the MPC is very specific about mental requirements:

- **Purposely.** Accused intended the action.
- **Knowingly.** Accused knew the outcome was certain but continued anyway.
- **Recklessly.** Accused knew the outcome was likely but did it anyway.
- **Negligently.** Accused should have known the outcome was likely.
- **Strict liability.** Accused's mental state is irrelevant.

Depending on the severity of the crime, jurisdictions that follow the MPC approach require the demonstration of different mental states depending on the severity of the crime. For example, parking violations are generally strict liability, whereas first-degree murder requires purpose.

Circumstances

Just because someone satisfies the actus reus and mens rea conditions of a crime does not always mean the defendant should be found criminally liable. There are also the elements of justification and excuse. Justification refers to actions that are technically a crime, but are justified under the circumstances. For example, if someone breaks into your house at night and you shoot him, causing his death, you have killed him (actus reus) and you intended to kill him (mens rea). Nonetheless, in this case the crime is deemed justified since it was in self-defense. This is not to say you always have the right to shoot an intruder; it must be justified. Someone who shoots a fleeing robber in the back would be found guilty in many states. The doctrine of excuse is used when an action is not justified, but the person nonetheless should not be held liable. The insanity defense is a form of excuse, although in reality, this method is really just another way of saying the individual did not have the required mens rea.

Minors

Eighteen is the magic number for the court's determination of adulthood. What age makes a person accountable in juvenile courts, however, has been difficult for all states to agree on. Although anyone under seven years of age is not generally held accountable for a crime, and those over the age of fourteen, however, will most likely face juvenile court if they commit crimes, for a person between the ages of seven and fourteen the pendulum could swing either way. In these situations, judgments are made based on the specific circumstances and mental state of the child.

Punishment

All crimes are not created equal. You will never be punished in the same way for a minor crime as you would for a serious crime. Imagine if you were to only pay a fine for committing a murder, or if you were to face lethal injection for a stolen library book. These two examples might seem extreme, but that is probably because you are already so immersed in the U.S. criminal system that the division between a felony and a misdemeanor is clear in your mind. Somewhere along the line you learned that murder is worse than stealing, and stealing is worse than parking next to a fire hydrant. But where does this hierarchy of crimes come from? Along with the apparent moral implications inherent in our legal system, there are concerns of practicality and safety that play into the ways we determine punishment. As put best by Gilbert and Sullivan, "let the punishment fit the crime."

- **Felony.** A felony is a serious crime. A felony will result in a large fine and/or a year or more in prison, depending on the state.
- **Misdemeanor.** A misdemeanor is a less serious crime than a felony. It will result in a fine or a year or less in prison, depending on the state. States have different definitions of what separates a felony from a misdemeanor. Marijuana is currently a hot topic regarding this distinction between states. Depending on the amount in a person's possession, some states might consider the crime a felony while others might consider it a misdemeanor. States refer to these types of offenses as "wobblers" since they teeter between felony and misdemeanor in classification.
- **Previous record and offenses.** No criminal case exists in a vacuum; your record lasts forever. There is no tabula rasa after you commit a crime, and your past actions will come back to haunt you if you go on to commit another one. At the same time, the reliance on records also protects those who have a clean history with the legal system. Consider if a person who stole every few years was judged in the same manner as a person who stole one time. If you have a criminal history it could change your misdemeanor into a felony. On the other hand, if you have a clean record, it could change a felony into a misdemeanor.

PRE-ARRAIGNMENT

Booking

If you are suspected of committing a crime, you will be arrested by the state. Whether or not you will be able to leave the jail will depend on your ability to meet bail.

Bail

Bail is the money given to the state for a detainee's temporary release from prison before and during the trial. Bail is not granted for all suspected criminals. For instance, the 1984 enactment of Title 18 of the U.S. Code mandates that a person suspected of being a danger to the community will not be allowed bail. This law replaced the Bail Reform Act of 1966, which was primarily concerned with the suspicion of suspect flight. States determine who is granted bail and who is not. States also determine whether a suspect will have to pay bail at all. In certain circumstances a person can promise to appear at court based on his or her *own recognizance.* Such a person is typically respected in the community and has a clean record. While the states have a great deal of control over the determination of bail, they are subject to the Constitution's Eighth Amendment, which prohibits excessive bail, along with excessive fines and cruel and unusual punishment. You can easily see the open-ended nature of these terms. Who determines what is "excessive"? What you think is excessive and what the court deems excessive may not match. Thus, this law has been under considerable scrutiny among courts and states.

ARRAIGNMENT

The first stage of criminal procedure is known as arraignment. As you read through the criminal trial procedures you may wish to consider the similarities and differences between these and the civil procedures.

Trial Procedure

- **Reading of charges.** A judge will read the charges to the person suspected of the crime, now officially known as the defendant.
- **Determination of legal representation.** The judge will ask the defendant if he or she has legal representation and will appoint a public attorney if the defendant is not able to procure representation.
- **Entering a plea.** The defendant will enter one of the following pleas: guilty, not guilty, or no contest.

- **Review of bail.** The judge will determine the bail or review it if it has already been given. The judge may change the bail or grant the defendant his or her own recognizance.

Trial Schedule

- **Preliminary hearing.** The preliminary hearing will determine whether the case needs to go to trial. A judge will determine this based on the amount of evidence against the defendant. The hearing does not determine whether the defendant is guilty or not guilty but whether there are sufficient grounds to continue the proceedings.
- **Pre-trial motions.** During the pre-trial motions the defense and the prosecution are given a chance to argue for and against the evidence being used against the defendant. For instance, if there is a witness who claims to have seen the defendant murder his wife, but the witness is legally blind, the defense will make a motion to exclude that witness from trial.
- **Discovery process.** The defense has the right to discover the prosecution's information before the trial. This is also known as *disclosure.* The prosecution also has the right to discover information from the defense. There are exceptions to both types of disclosure. For instance, the defense has the right to attorney-client privilege and the prosecution does not have to show certain confidential government documents to the general public.
- **Trial date set.** The judge will set the date for the trial, (usually) allowing sufficient time for both sides to prepare for the case but with an eye to a defendant's right to a speedy trial.

TRIAL

The procedure of the trial is heavily influenced by the concept of *standard of proof.* The standard of proof, or burden of proof, is upon the prosecution. The defense does not have to prove anything; it is up to the prosecution to prove without any reasonable doubt that the defendant is guilty of the crime. The criminal legal procedure is therefore set up to favor the defense. Practice, of course, is far different.

Judge or Jury Trial

In criminal proceedings, the defense may choose a judge or jury to determine the judgment.

Jury Selection

If a jury is chosen as the method for the defendant's judgment, the prosecution and defense will choose from a pool of citizens and determine whether they are all impartial toward the case. The jury will be expected to make decisions based on the evidence provided by the prosecution. The jury selection process is difficult because of the rather shaky definition of impartiality. There is not a single person in the world who has no previously formed ideas about certain people or situations, and the best the court can do is retain those with the least tendency toward prejudice.

Trial Steps

Following is the order of the steps in a trial.

- **Opening statements.** The prosecution and defense will present each of their arguments to the jury.
- **Prosecution presents case.** The prosecution will present evidence and witnesses to the jury.
- **Cross-examination.** The defense will examine the evidence and the witnesses.
- **Defense presents case.** The defense will present its evidence and witnesses.
- **Cross-examination.** The prosecution will examine the defense's evidence and witnesses.
- **Redirect.** The prosecution and defense will be given another opportunity to examine the evidence and witnesses.
- **Prosecution rests.** Once all the evidence has been presented and all the witnesses have been cross-examined, the prosecution will rest, or finish presenting and cross-examining.

- **Defense rests.** Once the evidence has been presented and the witnesses cross-examined, the defense will rest.
- **Closing arguments.** Both sides will give their final statements about the case. This is a good time to reevaluate the entire proceeding. Often there will be a critique of the methods used by the opposing counsel. There might be a summary of the events and a plea to the jury for a favorable verdict.
- **Jury instructions.** The judge will instruct the jury to reach a verdict in a private meeting room.
- **Deliberations.** The jurors must select a chairperson to speak for the group. During deliberations, the jury is allowed to speak candidly about the case and the trial.
- **Verdict.** The jury must come to a unanimous decision. If no decision can be made, a condition known as a hung jury, a mistrial will be declared, which usually means a new trial process must begin.
- **Post-trial motions.** If the jury has reached a verdict, the final word still may not have been spoken. Three types of motions can be made: *motion for judgment notwithstanding the verdict, motion for a new trial,* and *motion to alter or amend the judgment.* A motion for judgment notwithstanding the verdict asks the judge to overturn the jury's verdict. This rarely occurs since it insists that the evidence was so clearly in favor of the moving party that the verdict must be invalidated. A motion for a new trial usually occurs if one side finds some fault with the procedure—for instance, if a jury member is found to be improperly partial. A motion to alter or amend the judgment does not ask for a complete reversal but that a lesser change be made in the judgment.

SENTENCING

The governing principle of criminal law is punishment. The sentencing stage addresses the punishment of the now legally defined criminal. There are a number of forms of punishment, some much more appealing than others. The punishment of prison time is justified on a number of grounds. Imprisonment both protects the community from the criminal and allows the criminal a chance for rehabilitation. Obviously, there are differing views on the effectiveness of the U.S. penal system, but if your client has any chance of receiving a prison sentence, you are well advised to do research on the state's rehabilitation plans.

Sentencing Alternatives

- Suspended sentence
- Probation
- Fines
- Restitution
- Community service

The decision to opt for one of these alternatives to sentencing may be based on a number of factors. For instance, just as the amount of bail or nature of the hearing is determined by your record, the sentence you receive is based on your past actions. A first-time offender will not be punished as heavily as a repeat offender. A repeat offender is likely to receive a still harsher sentence in some states if the crime constitutes the "third strike," that is, the defendant has committed three crimes of a similar nature.

APPEALS

A court's decision still is not final until the appeals process. Although this procedure can take a long time, it gives the defendant a chance to receive a more favorable judgment. An appeal of a criminal judgment may include a *direct appeal* or a *collateral attack* through the *writ of habeas corpus.* A direct appeal allows the defendant to appeal to the next highest court. A collateral attack through the writ of habeas corpus is an appeal to the federal court. *Habeas corpus* is Latin for "you should have the body." The writ of habeas corpus asks the court to reexamine the case based on the defense's claim that something was missing or misunderstood in the proceedings.

SUMMATION

Knowing the context surrounding matters of criminal law is essential to communicating effectively in criminal court. A lawyer who treats writing for a criminal case in the same way as for a civil case will be unpleasantly surprised, but one who understands the varied roles that writing plays in criminal law will be able to use words to the advantage of both case and client. Before the bench and behind the desk, every case is won by clear, insightful communication that carries the logical and rhetorical force necessary to help ensure that justice is done.

Chapter 4

Transactional Drafting

THERE IS A TENDENCY TO characterize lawyers as a bunch of combatants all fighting to get in the last word. This adversarial relationship is certainly a strong influence in some of the legal writing you will be doing, but it is not the spirit you wish to convey when you are writing to commemorate an agreement or promise. This chapter explores an area of law that receives inadequate attention and deserves much more emphasis: transactional drafting.

IN THIS CHAPTER	
• **Principles of Transactional Drafting** ◦ Examples • **Contracts and Settlement Agreements** ◦ Contracts ◦ Settlement Agreements	◦ Procedural Guidelines for Drafting Contracts • **Trusts and Wills** ◦ Guidelines for Drafting a Trust ◦ Guidelines for Drafting a Will • **Summation**

PRINCIPLES OF TRANSACTIONAL DRAFTING

Transactional drafting demands clarity and objectivity rather than persuasion. Transactional drafting must be clear because it will generate direct results from its own words. This form of writing is very much like a script that an actor must perform word for word. The written document must tell the reader what to do, and the reader must then perform those actions. The worst-case scenario for an actor who cannot perform from the script may be a career teaching drama rather than working on Broadway. If a legal document is misinterpreted or just ignored, the consequences include litigation. When you work with transactions, the last thing you want to do is go to court. If the parties in a written agreement end up going to trial, it is a good bet the original draft was badly written.

Examples

The four types of transactional drafts discussed here are contracts, trust documents, wills, and settlement agreements.

- A *contract* is a legally binding agreement between two or more parties.
- A *settlement agreement* is intended to handle disputes between two or more parties.
- A *will* allows an individual to give rights in personal possessions or property to others at the time of the testator's death.
- A *trust* allows one party to handle the property of another individual.

The four types of transactional drafts all rely on a clear and methodical form in order to minimize the gap between meaning and interpretation. Think of any misunderstood phrases, books, articles, or even people you are familiar with. What is it that makes them unclear? Mark Twain once said the difference between the right word and the wrong word is like the difference between lightning and a lightning bug. Consider how using the wrong word in a contract or will could completely distort your intentions and your client's wishes. Transactional drafting is not an opportunity to write flowery prose or use broad language. Those abilities might come in handy in preparing an editorial piece but they are not at all helpful to your client. In fact, if there is any confusion, courts often give the benefit of the doubt to the party that did not draft the document. This form of legal writing requires a painstaking adherence to form and close observance of the writing that has preceded your own.

Keep in mind that contracts and trusts are representative of the common law system. As discussed in Chapter 1 with regard to the court system, drafts fall in a long line with all that have historically come before. Common law insists on the acknowledgment of precedent for both written and oral agreements. Consider reading the documents presently in circulation; such immersion can help you internalize the prevailing style of legal writing. For instance, it was once popular for lawyers to write in legalese, using Latin as often as possible; now there is a trend toward a simpler and more accessible style. But legal writing still has *terms of art*, which basically means lawyer-speak, that could confuse anyone who is not familiar with the jargon.

CONTRACTS AND SETTLEMENT AGREEMENTS

Contracts and settlement agreements are discussed in tandem here because these two types of transactional drafts are very closely related. A settlement is a contract since both are inherently agreements. Whereas a contract encompasses a much wider range of possible agreements, a settlement amounts to an agreement to settle a disagreement. As a citizen of the world you engage in a never-ending series of contracts with other individuals and groups. Any time you give money in exchange for a product, such as buying this book from a cashier, you are a party to a contract. The contract involved in buying a book, however, is an oral one. Written contracts represent the daily promises and agreements that you make with people.

Contracts

Contracts are a vital part of the American economy. Reliance on written contracts grew considerably in the early nineteenth century, as Adam Smith's economic theory became the driving force behind the nation's business strategies. Historically, an important concept underlying contracts is *adequate consideration.* Adequate consideration is a motivational device for the party receiving the promise in the contract. Adequate consideration may take the form of a benefit or detriment to the receiving party, but it must cause the party to make the promise. In terms of a formula:

- Promise + Adequate Consideration = Legally Binding Contract

There is a certain "quid pro quo" element to classic contracts that goes hand in hand with a market economy. Indeed, some of the most famous contract cases are related to buying and selling. For example, in *Mumford v. M'Pherson* (1806) there is an interesting lesson to be learned about the importance of a written contract and the consideration given to it over outside evidence. The buyer in this case said that he had been orally promised a ship with copper fastenings of a certain type, and that was not what was given to him by the seller. The bill of sale contained no promise of a copper fastening type, and the buyer did not win his case. The reason the buyer did not win is the *parol evidence rule*, which bars outside evidence from trumping what is in the final written contract. You can imagine how troubled the market would be if the word of the buyer were allowed to decide the outcome of a case on the price of material goods. Similar chaos would ensue if customers at a department store were permitted to use a coupon after the expiration date. Anyone who has ever used a coupon is aware of the fine print across the bottom that explains the contractual agreement on dates of use, exceptions to the sale, and any other types of exclusions. Fine print might annoy customers, but it creates certainty and it's a prime example of a basic contract that you come in contact with all the time.

Settlement Agreements

Whereas a contract prevents a dispute between parties, a settlement agreement ends a dispute between parties. A contract commemorates an understanding between parties and often regulates future behavior. Typically, settlement agreements resolve an existing disagreement by distributing assets. They may be forward looking, requiring future actions to complete the terms of the agreement. Settlement agreements may also incorporate other contracts. A common example of a settlement agreement is a divorce settlement. A divorce exemplifies the potentially hostile relationship between the parties involved in a settlement agreement. Like any other contract, a settlement agreement depends on a bargain between the two parties to create a legally binding instrument.

Procedural Guidelines for Drafting Contracts

- **Identify the parties.** The first step in creating a contract is to identify whom the contract is between. Once you know the parties involved you can determine the purpose of the contract. It's important not to exclude anyone who could be affected by the contract. For instance, imagine a contract between two companies over a shared property that was also shared by a third party. If that third party was not revealed in the contract and the companies built on this land, the parties to the contract would be involved in future dispute. So as simple as it might sound to know who is involved, resist the temptation to skip the specification of information you might consider obvious.
- **Determine the parties' rights and responsibilities.** Once you have established the people involved in the contract and its purpose, you need to determine each side's rights and responsibilities. This step in the contract requires as much specificity as possible. For instance, if you were drafting a contract for a house to be built, you would not want to be vague on the time frame. If you were writing a contract for a division of property, you would need to itemize each piece of property in possession of both parties.
- **Remedies.** The parties involved in the contract may not be able to fulfill all of their responsibilities. You must then provide remedies, or alternative plans, for those parts of the contract that cannot be met. For instance, if a contract demands that an individual work Monday through Friday, for forty hours a week, but the worker cannot come in on Tuesdays, a possible remedy might be for the worker to come in on Saturdays instead. A remedy is a plan B option.

- **State laws.** Often it is important to establish which state's law governs the contract. Being aware of the differences between states' laws is just another example of the importance of precision when it comes to drafting transactions.
- **Alternative dispute resolution.** As a rule, you do not want to go to court over a contract. One way to avoid the lengthy and costly avenue of litigation is to construct a mode of alternative dispute resolution within the contract. A binding arbitration, for example, may allow the parties to streamline dispute resolution. You may want to advise your client to include a dispute resolution clause contemplating either mediation or arbitration. Either of these vehicles for dispute resolution may simplify the resolution of a future dispute but it also, generally eliminates any right of appeal. Only your client can determine whether such a provision is in his or her best interest.
- **Broad to specific.** You will most likely be following the standardized form of jurisdiction for your particular type of contract. Think of this jurisdiction as a template to be adapted to fit your specific needs. This cannot be mentioned enough times: specificity is the key to a well-crafted contract.
- **Compliance with applicable law.** There is always the possibility that a part of your contract may go against the applicable law. This can occur due to your own carelessness or oversight, but the consequences are severe. As a form of insurance, write a statement that will allow you to keep the lawful parts and eliminate the unlawful ones. Rather than throwing out the whole contract, you can revise and correct your mistakes by having this safety net of provisions.
- **Party participation.** (This sounds more fun than it is.) All the parties must be given the opportunity to participate in the drafting process. Allow all parties to review the final contract.
- **Record keeping.** Stay organized throughout the drafting process. Hold on to all your records, which might include

e-mails, letters, rough drafts, and so forth. These documents might become necessary later to shed light on the intentions of both parties.

- **Be aware of public policies.** Each form of contract has its own rules and regulations. Be aware of them, and don't use one form of a contract with the wrong type of content. Using the wrong form could negate the legitimacy of your contract. The issue is the "enforceability" of the contract. If a contract is found to go against public policy, it will not be enforced

TRUSTS AND WILLS

Trusts and wills are a different breed of transactional draft from contracts and settlement agreements. Contracts rely on an agreement between parties; trusts and wills do not. Trusts and wills are about one person's wishes: the person drafting the document.

Trusts and wills are concerned with property rights. Property in this context does not just refer to the land a person lives on. Instead, think of property as anything in the possession of the individual who is drafting the trust or will. A *trust* is an arrangement where one person's property is under the control of the *trustee*, and may be set up during life or triggered by death. The trustee does not own the person's property but does have power over it. This might seem like a subtle difference, and indeed, many familial disputes are caused by the way trusts are set up.

A *will* indicates how an individual's property is to be disposed of at the time of the individual's death.

Guidelines for Drafting a Trust

- Identify all the parties and properties involved in the trust.
- Identify the term of the trust. (The term refers to how long the trust will last.)
- Identify what the trustee can and cannot do with the property. Be specific in stating these conditions, just as you would be with a contract.
- Be aware of the regulations concerning the trust. Often a trust must be notarized and/or formally recorded.

Guidelines for Drafting a Will

- Identify all the parties and properties involved in the will.
- Make it clear that the will you are drafting supersedes all previous wills.
- Be aware of the regulations governing the will. Like a trust, a will may need to be notarized and/or formally recorded.

The landmark case for trusts and wills is *Knight v. Knight* (1840). This case became important because it set up three ways to determine the validity of the documents. These stipulations are known as "the three certainties." The three certainties are intention, subject-matter, and objects.

- **Intention.** Determining one's intention in a trust is difficult if the correct wording is not used. The interpretation of intention in a trust therefore depends on the way the lawyer set up the trust. Once again this goes back to the importance of specific wording and the avoidance of ambiguity.
- **Subject matter.** The property is the subject matter. It is important to be specific about the exact property being drafted. A case that serves as a good example of how *not* to write a trust is *Palmer v. Simmonds* (1854). In this trust, the term "bulk" was used to refer to the estate. It was deemed insufficient for describing how much of the estate would go into the trust.
- **Object.** The object of the trust is also known as the beneficiary. Being specific about whom the trust is for helps to prevent the trustee from being charged with fraud.

Although it is a bit premature to discuss grammar, you should note that the drafting of a trust looks like your basic sentence diagram:

- **Trustee** (subject) **intends** (verb) **subject matter** (direct object) for the **beneficiary** (indirect object).

SUMMATION

Although the actual drafting of transactions can be challenging, the principles that govern their writing are actually pretty easy to remember. Be specific with every aspect of your drafts; contracts, settlement agreements, wills, and trusts demand acute attention to detail. Remember that you are creating a template of rules to govern future behavior. These rules are a part of the larger body of law that makes up the U.S. legal system and are always subject to it. As you write these rules think about how you would want your own property to be treated. Think about the possible confusion that faulty word choices could cause. Your writing is the last line of defense for communication and understanding between the parties involved. Remember, you do not want to go to court over a badly written transactional document.

Chapter 5

Legal Research

YOU HAVE LEARNED ABOUT SOME of the basic areas of law, and you probably have noticed that in both civil and criminal procedures there is a research stage that requires the lawyer to examine the case in the light of the common law and legislative history preceding it. Lawyers are required to be familiar with all of the statutes and case matter that might influence the case at hand. They also must have an understanding of how jurisdiction dictates which sources will control the case and which ones will merely guide arguments. Having a clear methodical strategy as you enter the research stage of your case might be what keeps you a step ahead of your opposing counsel.

IN THIS CHAPTER	
• **Research Strategy** ◦ What Is the Legal Problem? ◦ Developing a Strategy • **Types of Resources** ◦ Primary Authorities ◦ Secondary Authorities	• **Research Tools** • **Methods of Access** • **Summation**

RESEARCH STRATEGY

Have you ever tried to research and write a paper the night before the assignment was due? Perhaps you are one of those rare individuals who work well under pressure and can succeed in writing last-minute research papers. On the other hand, you might have a tendency toward procrastination, or maybe you take writing less seriously than other types of work. Perhaps you just avoid such assignments until the last minute because you don't trust your writing skills. Developing a research strategy can help relieve such misgivings and redirect your energy in a more productive direction.

Last-minute writing is to be avoided in the legal arena. Legal writing is often done for a client, and the client deserves your best work. Writing intelligently about a multitude of legal issues requires significant research, conscientious application of that research, and the use of the proper writing style to ensure your arguments are convincing.

What Is the Legal Problem?

Before you begin your research, you must pinpoint the question you need to answer. You have a legal problem to solve, and it helps to articulate that problem to yourself in your own words. If you are having difficulty phrasing the legal issue, it may be helpful to write a short, descriptive sentence about your research goals before you begin. This will help you to focus and clear your thoughts. Legal issues can be confusing and convoluted, and it is important to make your goals clear before you begin. Once you have defined the legal problem, you can begin devising a strategy to address it.

Developing a Strategy

As you begin to determine your research strategy, you must be both organized and adaptable. These might seem like contradictory objectives, but balancing them can keep you ahead of the curve and reduce the intense pressure that comes with being a lawyer.

Organization

Before you begin your research, it's wise to prepare a plan of attack. A research schedule can keep you from procrastinating and allow you to set obtainable short-term goals. Be realistic about your own time constraints and how they relate to your required due dates. Keep your schedule in a prominent place where you can't ignore it. If you're always at your computer, iCalendar software might work for you. If you prefer using highlighters and markers, a large wall calendar might be better.

It is also helpful to take careful notes when reading through the various relevant authorities. Some legal issues might require you to become familiar with a large number of cases. Some people find it helpful to keep track of case names, holdings, and fact patterns during research. This can be done through informal note taking, or by using a spreadsheet program. Not only will this help you to keep a record of what research you have completed, but it also provides a useful means of comparing and distinguishing case law based on holdings and fact patterns. This can be an invaluable tool when you begin to draft your brief or memo. Another thing to keep track of is the current state of any authority you find. Always remember that the law is constantly changing. What is binding authority one day can be overturned the next. For each relevant case you find, write down a brief description of the facts, the holding, and whether or not it has been followed, distinguished, or overturned.

Adaptability

As much as you need to be organized with respect to your research schedule, you need to be prepared for unexpected events. Sometimes a case will fall into your lap and require immediate attention and research efforts. You'll have to learn to roll with the punches you'll inevitably receive as an associate. Make sure you budget sufficient time not only to finish your current project, but also to allow for additional tasks.

The art of adaptability requires flexibility and resilience. Your research strategy should adapt to each situation, but it will always depend on three things: your knowledge of the area, your own goals, and your comfort level with the various types of research tools. This can be restated as what you know, what you need to know, and how you find it out. The less experience you have as a legal researcher, the less knowledge you will be coming in with, which will make what you need to know all the more daunting.

TYPES OF RESOURCES

- **Recognizing your sources.** There are two basic sources of legal research: primary authorities and secondary authorities. You may be familiar with the two types of research authorities from your previous education. Recognizing the difference between the two as you sift through various documents is a bit more difficult than knowing their basic definitions. Primary and secondary authorities are discussed in detail below.
- **Locating your sources.** With the technology now available, you have many choices in the methods of research to use. You can use online case searches, digests, treatises, restatements, practice guides, and law review articles. Using a citation service such as *KeyCite* or *Shepard's* will keep you from overlooking any relevant history.

Primary Authorities

Laws and case law constitute primary authorities. Judicial opinions and statutes are examples of primary authorities. Using a primary source will require you to determine its meaning and how it fits your case's needs. Remember, not all case law and statutes in an area will be equally relevant to your needs. Just because you find a court of appeals decision that directly relates to your legal issue does not mean it will be binding on your jurisdiction; it might be simply *persuasive* authority. For instance, if you have a case in the 5th Circuit and you uncover a decision by the 6th Circuit that relates to the issue involved in the case, the decision will not be binding on the 5th Circuit court, but it might persuade it. Primary authority that is binding upon your jurisdiction is known as controlling authority. There is little more embarrassing than crafting an argument around inapplicable authority when controlling precedent exists.

Keep in mind that primary authorities are the actual sources of law. The three sources of law you must be familiar with are legislation, judicial opinions, and administrative rules. Following is a list of these categories with examples for each.

- **Legislation.** These resources are created by the legislature.
  - Constitutions. The Constitution of the United States of America is the key document of the nation and also the most difficult primary source to explicate. There are other primary interpretive sources to use when you use the Constitution. The United States Supreme Court is the first interpreter of the Constitution to consult. The history of Supreme Court cases is lengthy and complex due to the various opinions and commentaries provided. West's United States Code Annotated (U.S.C.A), the United States Code Service, and the Library of Congress Edition of the Constitution are good examples of primary sources for researching and interpreting the Constitution.
  - Statutes
  - International treaties and conventions
  - County and city codes, charters, ordinances, etc.
- **Judicial opinions.** These opinions are created by federal, state, and local systems. These systems are divided into three levels:
  - Highest court
  - Intermediate appellate courts: circuit courts.
  - Trial courts: district courts.
- **Administrative rules.** These include court rules and regulations, decrees, orders, licenses, and interpretations of executive and administrative and/or regulatory agencies. These rules exist mainly because it is too

difficult to create new laws for every regulation that needs to be enforced.

When you are looking through primary sources it is important to consider the *text* you are reading within its particular *context*. The text refers to the document itself whereas the context refers to how the language of that document is meant to be interpreted. For example, if you are reading a statute that discusses the term "tomato" and the statute defines a tomato as a vegetable, you would need to do the same even though we all know, outside the context of that statute, a tomato is a fruit.

Secondary Authorities

A secondary authority is not a controlling source and should never be used in place of primary authorities. Secondary sources help explain the connections between primary authorities and may even rehash what the primary authority says. Secondary authorities are helpful in translating primary authorities, but, like a translation of the *Iliad* into the English language, a secondary source will never provide all the facts and nuances present in the primary authority.

An important feature of a secondary authority is that it is *persuasive* authority. A secondary authority may be persuasive but it will never be controlling. It is important to remember that a secondary authority can be a useful place to begin your research. Although it can never be used as controlling authority in your brief, it can serve as a roadmap to help you locate relevant primary authority. There are often jurisdiction-specific sources that provide a useful summary of legal issues, lists of the primary authorities most often cited, as well as recent changes in the law. Secondary authorities help interpret the law and might help you understand a general area of the law better. If you have difficulty finding a primary authority dealing with your legal issue, a secondary authority can be invaluable.

Examples of secondary authorities follow.

- **Law journal articles.** These scholarly articles can be quite valuable as resources; however, keep in mind that the authors are often making prescriptive arguments about what the law should be rather than dealing with its reality.

- **Treatises.** These are academic resources about the law. They are analytical, interpretive, and expository. In any given area there tends to be one well-regarded treatise that has become established by its reputation. Examples of treatises range from generic legal treatises, such as student hornbooks, to treatises specific to a jurisdiction, such as the law in California.
- **Restatements.** These are authoritative statements of the law in a particular area. They are generally a reliable source of authority.
- **Legal encyclopedias and legal dictionaries.** These are valuable resources, but you don't want to use them too much in your writing if other primary authorities are available. The inclusion of a legal dictionary as the main source in your legal writing could look under-researched. In the absence of other authority, however, such definitions can be quite useful.

RESEARCH TOOLS

Following are some famous services to use as you begin your legal research.

- **Citation services.** The most common citation service is *Shepard's.* Frank Shepard devised this system for organizing cases in 1873, and now the verb "to shepardize," which refers to the process of verifying cases, honors his name. These citations are available in book or online form, through Lexis. There is also *KeyCite,* which is available only online. *KeyCite* is *Shepard's* true competitor since it has some capabilities that *Shepard's* lacks. Both *Shepard's* and *KeyCite* compile the subsequent history of a case or statute, stating if it has been overturned, repealed, or modified in some way. They also find other cases that have followed its ruling. Both *Shepard's* and *KeyCite* are great starting points, but remember to actually read the cases they bring up.

- **Digests and annotations.** These research aids compile a set of resources organized by "headnote" or theme. Although digests have been largely replaced by online searches, they are a good alternative when technology lets you down. Annotated law reports are articles that gather cases and other resources surrounding a specific topic.

METHODS OF ACCESS

Despite the common image of attorneys as individuals crouched over law books, today the legal profession relies heavily on professional search engines such as *Westlaw* and *Lexis.* These methods of research have some benefits over book research. First, they can be updated instantly whenever a new case is decided, a new statute is enacted, or an old statute is repealed or amended. This enables the legal community to stay apprised of legal changes whenever they occur. Second, it is now possible to do natural language searches rather than browse through indexes. This enables the researcher to locate relevant information more quickly. Finally, once you locate relevant authority, you can immediately examine the case history to determine its relevancy to your case.

To effectively search a substantive legal issue, however, a lawyer must understand the legal backdrop. This enables the lawyer to use the right terms in an online search engine. A treatise or other secondary authority provides the lever to lift the rock. Over-reliance on computer-based research is the single worst mistake a young associate can make. Using online resources exclusively in legal research often amounts to "garbage in, garbage out." It is important to use the various research tools in a complementary fashion.

With the availability of effective on-line research, it is important to become a knowledgeable and efficient Internet user. To make effective use of a citation service, digest, or annotation you need to know where to look. Toward this end there are a few methods at your disposal, each with its own costs and benefits.

- **Online Westlaw and Lexis.** These online tools are fee-based, but the reason for the payments becomes obvious when you realize how much better Westlaw and Lexis are than other methods of online research. They contain a majority of the resources you will need, including statutes, cases, regulations, law journals, and treatises. Westlaw or Lexis will almost always be your first step in a research project. They are expensive, but losing a case because you failed to do the research is a much higher price to pay.

- **Online free search engines and databases.** Findlaw and the Cornell Legal Information Institute provide free information. Unfortunately, the information is not nearly as comprehensive as that provided by Westlaw and Lexis.
- **The law library.** Another free source is the library. Older resources are also more likely to be available at a law library than on online databases.

SUMMATION

Remember that it will take a great deal of practice to become proficient in legal research. Do not despair when you find yourself lost in the sheer volume of cases with a key search term. It might help to keep John Keats' concept of negative capability in mind as you begin to doubt your research skills: being in a state of uncertainty will guide you toward greater insight in time.

Chapter 6

Interpreting Statutes and Cases

AS YOU MIGHT REMEMBER FROM Chapter 5, statutes and cases are primary authorities for you to use in your legal writing. They are also the most common types of authority you will find throughout your research. As you read this chapter, keep in mind that statutes and case decisions are simply rules to follow. However, misunderstanding or misinterpreting a statute or case could very well hurt your professional career as a lawyer. Interpreting cases and statutes is a process that every lawyer must master.

IN THIS CHAPTER	
• **Statutory Construction** ◦ Legislative Power ◦ A Statute's Language ◦ Clarifying the Text ◦ Helpful Sources ◦ Research Strategies	• **Cases** ◦ Determining the Rule of a Case ◦ The Structure of a Case ◦ Finding the Rule ◦ Identifying the Dicta • **Summation**

STATUTORY CONSTRUCTION

Although statutes have been identified in earlier chapters, as a refresher we will review the basic definition and, more important, how that definition depends on the construction of the statute. Indeed, what defines a statute is the way it is created and by whom it is created.

Legislative Power

Statutes are rules created by a body empowered with legislative authority. Legislative authority is the power to make laws. Here are some examples of statutes:

- **Federal laws.** These are the laws passed by Congress. They must be enacted by both the House of Representatives and the Senate, and then signed by the president. The Constitution provides Congress with very specific powers, such as the power to legislate interstate commerce. The general trend in recent times has been to give a broad reading to the powers bestowed on Congress.
- **State laws.** These are laws passed by a state legislature. Every state other than Nebraska has a bicameral congress similar to the federal Congress.
- **Municipal/county ordinances.** These are laws passed by city or county councils. Cities and counties generally have a municipal code that contains these laws, and they are enforced along with state and federal laws.

The following are similar to statutes but are not considered exactly the same as statutes because of differences in their construction.

- **International treaties.** These are agreements between nations that can be enacted as soon as they are written. In the United States, some treaties are entered into solely via executive agreement, whereas others require approval by two-thirds of the Senate or sometimes a simple majority of Congress. The president has the ability to enter into an international agreement, but might seek the support of the Congress if the treaty involves additional federal legislation. It is important to be familiar with treaties because they carry the same force as statutes.

- **Administrative agency regulations.** Sometimes Congress will pass legislation creating agencies that exist outside the executive branch. The legislation will define the purpose of the agency, as well as its powers and its ability to make rules. Rules and regulations enacted by these independent agencies have the force of federal law within their prescribed areas. Basically, Congress bestows its rule-making ability in a specific area onto a specific agency. Examples are the Environmental Protection Agency and the Federal Trade Commission.
- **Executive orders.** An executive order is a directive made by the president of the United States or a governor of some state. When the president makes an executive order in conjunction with an act of Congress, the executive order has the force of law. There is some basis in the Constitution for presidential executive orders because the president has the power to enforce the laws. There is disagreement, however, over how far this power extends.

A Statute's Language

Some of the major controversies in our society are based on how different people interpret texts in opposing ways. The Bible is an obvious example of a controversial text; it has plethora of interpretations and is the object of heated contention. Statutes, or rules, may not generate as much controversy as the Bible, but they certainly produce a large amount of frustration and confusion among lawyers. In an ideal world, the meaning of a statute would be immediately understood by all of its readers. The reality is that the meaning of a statute is only as clear as the language it uses. The more difficult the language, the more likely it is the lawyer will spend a long time doing research to decipher its true meaning. Interpreting the language of statutes is a major part of working with the law.

Clarifying the Text

The language of a statute is the key piece of evidence for determining its meaning; thus, the primary goal in writing a statute should be *clarity*. The meaning of each term may not be clearly stated. One of the reasons statutes are so long-winded is that the writers do not want to leave anything out. Words may not have the same meanings in statutes as they do in common usage or dictionaries. The first step in interpreting a statute, then, is to look for a framework that will enable you to understand its terms. You will need to think of the potential interpretations that any given word or phrase could engender. Think about the difference between these two examples of directions:

- The chores must be done by 5.
- Daniel Smith must complete the following tasks by 5 p.m. on August 25 of 2008 for Karen Smith at 213 W. Tree Court in Smithfield, New Jersey: clean the kitchen floor using a mop and a bucket full of hot water with half a cup of soap.

Note that the second set of directions specifies who must complete the task and whom the task is for, where and when the task is to be carried out, the deadline, the means, and so forth. But also note that there is still room for differences in interpreting and satisfying these directions. If there are any questions or ambiguities, the rule is in trouble. The goal in preparing a statute is to keep questions and alternative interpretations to a minimum. It is virtually impossible, however, for a drafter to anticipate every factual circumstance that a statute might govern.

Here are some helpful tips to keep in mind if you plan on using a statute in your own legal writing:

- Find the section of the statute that is pertinent to your particular case. You must read the provision in keeping with its context.
- Determine a research strategy before you begin reading statutes. Having a method in mind can make reading

lengthy statutes less tedious by helping you avoid irrelevant sections.

- Pay attention to the definitions of terms. This cannot be stressed enough. No matter how certain you may be of a term's meaning, it will always benefit you to go the extra mile and discover other possible meanings.
- When you cite a provision, directly quote it. Never paraphrase a statute! It is the statute that governs, not your interpretation of it.

Helpful Sources

Despite all your best efforts, a statute's text is sometimes too ambiguous or too convoluted for you to unravel. The following sources will help clarify the meanings of statutes:

- Indications of *legislative intent.* Examples of these are committee findings, reports, floor debates, and amendment history.
- Court cases interpreting and applying a statute.
- Academic treatises and restatements.
- Commentaries and law review articles interpreting a statute.

Keep in mind that secondary sources are a starting point for research. Secondary sources are useful guides, but they are not the destination.

Research Strategies

- Write down your strategy before you begin hitting the books. You'll need to consider how much time you have to do the research. If you have a week to do research on statutes, your strategy will be different than if you have only two days. You also need to consider how much financial support you have at your disposal. Remember that Westlaw and other pay databases may charge you by the hour or some other time increment.
- Begin your research by reading the statutes. People have different reading speeds, but the objective is to do a close analysis of the language.

- Review annotations related to the statutes. Annotated versions of statutes are helpful because they list cases that might have modified the statutes by interpretation.
- Read the cases mentioned in the annotations. Focus on the aspects of the case that are relevant to your research rather than getting bogged down in all the details.
- Look for diverging opinions on statutes. If you notice sharp contrasts between authorities, research the legislative history of the statute.

CASES

Cases evolve from the cases that came before them. Unlike statutes, in which governing law is established by a legislative body with the intent of specifying a rule that applies in all potentially related situations, cases establish the relevant law based on the facts before that particular court on that particular day. Later cases interpret that decision—or *precedent*—and attempt to determine how the rule of the prior case should be applied to the facts before the present court. Often a significant amount of interpretation is involved, so that the common law could "evolve" in many different directions. In addition, statutes are subject to interpretation or "gloss" from reviewing courts. It is in these creative and varied interpretations of prior cases, and the persuasiveness of the associated arguments, that the "art" of law resides.

Determining the Rule of a Case

As a lawyer, one of your main duties will be to read and analyze cases relevant to the legal issue at hand. Becoming familiar with the facts of each case, as well as the legal rule, or *holding*, of each case will help you to present convincing arguments about how your legal issue should be resolved. The holding is a sentence or short discussion that explains the rules used to resolve the issues in the case.

There are also different types of *opinions* to consider and construe when you research the ruling of a case.

- **Unanimous opinion.** All the judges agree on the outcome of a case.

- **En banc opinion.** A large group of judges sat to hear the case, and a majority of the group agreed on the outcome of the case.
- **Majority opinion.** A majority of the judges on a court agree, making the opinion the rule of the case.
- **Plurality opinion.** The case resulted in a variety of different opinions, one of which received more votes than the others but not a majority of votes.
- **Concurring opinion.** This opinion agrees with the final decision but not with all of the reasoning behind it.
- **Dissenting opinion.** This opinion disagrees with the court's decision.
- **Per curiam opinion.** This opinion has no particular judge associated with it. It usually is a broader opinion, is generally accorded less precedential weight, and is often not published.

It's important to note that some cases don't result in a majority opinion. This could occur, for example, if a number of judges agree with the result but not the reasoning. In such a case, none of the opinions can be said to speak for the court as a whole.

Structure of a Case

A published opinion has three main parts:

- The facts and procedural history of the case
- An examination of the applicable law (statutes, prior cases, etc.)
- An application of existing law to the current case. This is the part that gives the rule.

Often a case involves more than one legal question, so there is the potential for multiple rules and discussion sections in a published opinion.

Note that opinions are written in an authoritative tone. Despite an opinion's rhetorical association with an editorial, a legal opinion usually maintains an emotional distance from the case.

Finding the Rule

The rule is usually found at the end of a case. The rule of a case is the proposition that will be applied to other cases. Some common forms of rules are the following.

- **Balancing test.** Two or more considerations are weighed against each other.
- **List of elements.** This takes the form of a logical proof: If *a*, *b*, and *c* are present, then the legal result will be *x*.
- **Adoption and modification.** Courts often adopt, modify, or apply rules borrowed from other cases. For example, the rule of case X may actually be a modification of a rule in case Y. This is known as a *borrowed rule*.

Identifying Dicta

Often, the text of a case can be quite long and will include writing not essential to the holding or the outcome. This writing is referred to as *dicta* and does not function as binding precedent on lower courts. For example, a court might be deciding a contract dispute and award damages to the plaintiff. The dicta might add that these damages might not be warranted if the situation had been different, and then give examples of possible ways other facts might have influenced the outcome. These speculations would be considered dicta, since they are not necessary to the reasoning behind the holding of the case. Although these statements might be used in persuasive writing if a conflict arises that was addressed by the court in its speculations, this would not be binding authority. Identifying dicta is one of the most difficult parts of interpreting cases. Here are some hints for finding dicta.

- If claims are hypothetical, they are dicta. An example of a hypothetical statement is "If fact X had not been present, the result might have been different."
- If claims are not a part of the court's reasoning in the case, consider them dicta.

Dicta represent the superfluous language in the text. It might help to color-code your cases to clearly distinguish the language germane to your argument and the dicta, which should be used only as a secondary source.

SUMMATION

As you write for the courtroom, much of your work will involve the statutes and court decisions that govern and illuminate your own cases. The work you put into understanding these materials and why they are written the way they are will have a direct impact on the integrity and persuasiveness of your own writing. A sure grasp of and thorough familiarity with statutory and case law can be the firm foundation on which to build your case and your career.

Chapter 7

Oral and Written Advocacy

SOME ADVOCATE THE PEDAGOGICAL METHOD of teaching people to write in the style in which they speak, so that the true voice of the writer is brought to the page. But what if you don't like the way you speak? Some people are mortally terrified of public speaking. The American educational system generally does little to train individuals in the art of spoken argument or even for logical written argument. If you are used to taking multiple-choice tests, presenting your arguments in oral or written form may be much more difficult than identifying the logical progressions underlying the answers. Writing is a private act, and this quality of isolation creates its own frustrations. Speaking is a public act, and it can intimidate lawyers because all of their mistakes are immediately open to the scrutiny of their colleagues and opponents, and to the judges, jury, and laypeople.

IN THIS CHAPTER

- **Importance of Oral and Written Advocacy**
- **Written Advocacy**
    - Types of Written Documents
    - General Principles
- **Oral Advocacy**
    - General Guidelines
    - Pretrial Argument
    - Oral Advocacy at Trial
- **Appellate Oral Advocacy**
    - Form
    - Preparing Your Argument
    - Making an Oral Argument
- **Summation**

IMPORTANCE OF ORAL AND WRITTEN ADVOCACY

Throughout the litigation process, from pleadings and pretrial motions on through appeals to the court of last resort, oral and written advocacy are the two basic tools of attorneys. They are certainly not mutually exclusive tools, and they actually will work in concert if you let them. Your argument style in briefs should be reflected in your oral arguments. You may feel more comfortable writing briefs than speaking in public forums, or vice versa, but ultimately you want to be competent in both arenas. You can improve only by making yourself repeat the process over and over. You will make mistakes, but don't let your insecurities and fears keep you from fine-tuning your craft. If you can master writing and speaking as a lawyer, you'll be surprised how much more comfortable you'll feel when you do those things in your everyday life.

WRITTEN ADVOCACY

At all stages of a case you will be submitting written documents. You simply cannot escape paperwork. The majority of your written work will occur before and after the trial.

Types of Written Documents

Following are the various types of documents you'll have to prepare.

- **Pleadings.** The first stage of a case is submitting your claims or defenses. As discussed in earlier chapters, the plaintiff will submit the complaint and the defendant will submit an answer.

- **Discovery requests.** Recall that the discovery stage occurs when you and your opposing counsel are collecting evidence and interviews from witnesses. You will need to submit written requests and subpoenas to receive information. You will also respond in writing to discovery requests.
- **Pretrial motions.** Motions are essentially any requests you might present to the court. These can range from asking for more time for you to prepare your case to motions for summary judgment (recall from Chapter 2 that a motion for summary judgment is a request for the judge to make a decision about the case before it goes to trial).
- **Motions for post-trial relief.** These are motions to change the result in an action.
- **Appellate briefs and writ applications.** These documents represent the first steps in the appeals process. They are written in a style intended to get the attention of the higher courts, and they tend to jump right into the main argument.

General Principles

Different chapters of this book cover the various types of writing you will encounter in litigation as well as transactional writing and objective writing. Each type of writing has its own requirements, but following are some general principles to be aware of.

- **Written advocacy should be formal.** When you write legal documents, try to avoid colloquialisms, or the kind of expressions that tend to be popular in everyday speech. You will be reading hundreds of cases during law school, so take advantage of your studies and consider the styles and formats of other lawyers.
- **Be assertive but not over-emotional.** Think about the difference between "I feel" and "one thinks" in a written piece. The former uses the first person singular with a clearly emotional verb. The latter conveys the distance of the third person singular and its verb refers to the cerebral process. Advocacy should concern itself with rational thoughts, not feelings. It's inevitable that you will often

have strong feelings and emotional reactions about your cases (you are human, after all), but your writing should not reflect those biases.

- **Be concise but thorough.** This might sound like a contradiction in terms. How can you write something with a lot of details and not manage to write too much? Choosing the proper structure and using economical language will help to frame your big ideas in simple formats. You will deal with complicated cases, but you don't need to write in a complicated style. Strive to narrow the gap between the reader and the writer.
- **Stay clear.** Law clerks generally have a limited amount of time to devote to reading documents, and time spent deciphering unclear writing is time lost. Avoid vague terms and ambiguous statements and use descriptive language with concrete characteristics. Consider the difference between the following sentences:
    - The man died in a tragic manner by means of a knife.
    - The plaintiff's father was stabbed three times in the chest and died five hours later from the internal injuries.

  The first sentence uses a vague subject, "the man," rather than a specific person in the case. It also uses the subjective adjective "tragic," which makes a judgment regarding the death of the man. It also includes "manner," which is a weak word with many meanings, making it hard to pin down. The second sentence is specific about the way the person died. It gives a detailed picture of what happened and the person it happened to. The description lets you see the case in your mind's eye.
- **Structure your presentation strategically to feature critical points**. Don't hide your main points at the end of your document. You should not focus most of your paper on the background of the case and neglect the major claims your case rests on. Don't forget that your opponent will be highlighting his or her own key points, so you need to anticipate possible problems with your own arguments as well as pointing out holes in those of your opponent.

ORAL ADVOCACY

At all stages, effective oral advocacy supplements, and sometimes replaces, written advocacy. The use of oral arguments allows judges to question attorneys directly and to probe the weaknesses in their briefs. Oral arguments also can provide clarification on ambiguous points in the briefs.

General Guidelines

- **Be respectful and courteous toward the judge and other parties.** "Respect" is a word that is tossed around a lot, but remember that the type of respect you should give depends on the kind of respect your audience demands. If your judge requests that you button your suit jacket, taking the jacket off and tossing it over your shoulder would be a sign of disrespect. If your jury consists of senior citizens, referring to "old people" in your opening statement may seem disrespectful to them. Context is key to knowing how to show respect.
- **Be punctual.** This is really just another form of respect, but one that doesn't change with the context. If you are someone who is always late, it's time to change this bad habit now. It is better to overcompensate and arrive early for every engagement. People rarely get upset if you are too early for a trial.
- **Be professional in dress and demeanor.**
- **Be well organized.**
- **Be thoroughly prepared.** Know exactly what you want to say and have all the materials you will need readily available.

Pretrial Argument

Hearings are often held on pretrial motions, venue, jury selection, and other stages of a trial. Usually these are less formal and ritualized than appellate oral arguments; therefore, there are no set time limits and typically there is more of a free-flowing conversation. The open-ended nature of these hearings can make it difficult to emphasize the points you want to make. You must master the art of legal conversation. Treat your case like a fascinating story you must share with the group. You do not want to appear to dominate or dictate, but you want to hit all the important points. Think of someone you know who manages to light up a room without trying to be the center of attention. It's certainly a tall order to become naturally charismatic, but if you can identify what is special about other people's conversation skills, you might be able to emulate them.

Oral Advocacy at Trial

Evidentiary and procedural hearings along with motions for post-trial relief are similar to pretrial arguments. They are much more discussion oriented and less structured than trials. At trial, the opening statement and closing argument are the bookends of the case. The opening statement should set up the main elements of your case. The closing argument summarizes the most important elements of your case and rebuts your opponent's case. Both arguments should be as clear and concise as possible. No one will respect your argument more just because of its length; size does not matter in this case.

You should be courteous but not to the point of timidity. Don't make apologies for your point of view, but recognize the perspectives of the audience and adapt your presentation to them. As discussed in earlier chapters, adaptation is an essential characteristic of a strong lawyer. You already adapt your tone in everyday conversations. Consider the language you use when you talk to your parents as opposed to the kind you use with your friends. Chances are you don't talk to your boss in the same way as you talk to your co-workers. This is due to your internal recognition of the power relationships between yourself and the people with whom you interact. You will most likely not talk to a judge in the exact same way as you will talk to a jury. And as you get to know the idiosyncrasies of different judges, you will not talk to all the judges in the same way either. Your legal research extends beyond statutes and cases. You need to know the way other people might approach your case.

APPELLATE ORAL ADVOCACY

Form

After both parties have filed their briefs, the court will have them come in for oral arguments. Each party will be given a certain amount of time to speak. During oral arguments, the judge will ask questions to clarify particular points. This is also a time for judges to debate those points with counsel. The goal in oral appellate advocacy is balancing the argument you wish to make with the questions the judge wants you to answer. A judge's persistent questions might sidetrack you from the big argument you want to make. Maintain a focus on your goals while also satisfying the judge's agenda. You will usually be arguing before a panel, which typically consists of three judges. In some contexts, such as the U.S. Supreme Court or an en banc rehearing, you will be addressing the whole court. (An en banc hearing occurs after a panel has ruled. The unsuccessful party can petition the entire court to hear the case and rethink the panel's decision.)

Preparing Your Argument

Know your legal authorities and the facts of your case backward and forward. Prepare a map or outline of the main points ahead of time. Don't write your entire argument out. If you are seen reading your entire argument off of a piece of paper, people are less likely to respect you and your argument. Moreover, it's unlikely that circumstances will remain fixed, and you will always need to make little (or big) adjustments throughout the argument. It will help, however, to plan a quick introduction so that you can cover all your main points before the questioning begins. It will also calm your nerves to know that the first part of your presentation is planned out. You should also prepare a very short (one or two sentences) conclusion emphasizing your strongest arguments. You should anticipate the most likely questions you will be asked and prepare answers to them. Here are some ways to prepare for those questions:

- Consider all the possible weaknesses in your case.
- Be aware of the areas in your argument where your language or ideas are not clear.
- Know your judges. Some judges might be more hostile toward your arguments than others. Some might have pet peeves with respect to an attorney's rhetoric.
- Anticipate alternative arguments. If you can recognize those alternatives and prepare a rebuttal to them, you will be in a much more comfortable position with regard to the argument.

Making an Oral Argument

One of the critical aspects of an oral argument is your tone. You do not want to sound like a sarcastic teenager or an Evangelical preacher when you are in a courtroom. If you have serious concerns over the way your voice sounds, it might help to tape-record yourself and practice different pronunciations of problem words or phrases. There is no shame in recognizing your own weaknesses as an orator. It would be much more shameful to fail to be respected as a speaker because of a quirk in your tone of voice. Tone does not refer just to your voice, however. When you walk into a courtroom, you set a tone without saying a word. Your expressions, mannerisms, and overall countenance determine the tone you establish. Here are some tips for setting the right tone:

- Be respectful but assertive. For example, you can disagree with a premise in a question asked by a judge, but respectfully disagree without being disagreeable. There are certain verbal cues that suggest both respect and assertiveness: "I see your point, but allow me to suggest the following" or "With all due respect, I have to disagree."
- Be professional in your demeanor and conservative in your attire. Fashion may be changing quickly in the new millennium, but the courtroom remains very old-school about what is and what is not appropriate dress. Ally McBeal might have gotten away with miniskirts, but you, likely, will not.
- Remember to keep your tone conversational rather than oratorical. You are not talking at or down to your judges, you are talking with them.
- Maintain a normal conversational speed and good eye contact with all your judges. Shifty eyes or the constant batting of your eyelashes will be taken the wrong way eventually.
- Don't ridicule or satirize an argument of your opponents. Be logical and assertive but never condescending.

When you are asked questions, consider these tips:

- Stop talking as soon as a judge starts asking a question. Do not talk over the judge even if he interrupts you. It's important to treat the judge with respect even if he does not seem to merit it. Your personal opinions about a judge are irrelevant, and it will only hurt your case if you let them determine your tone.
- Answer succinctly but be sure to include all relevant information.
- Do not concede important points.
- Try to make an effortless transition back to the flow of your main argument.

SUMMATION

Oral advocacy is more than merely contracting to win a case. It is agreeing to make every effort to see that justice is done. Whether in pleadings, discovery requests, or post-trial motions, your skill at oral and written communication is essential to presenting the full merit of your client's case. Obscuring your client's case with confusing wording and distracting personal statements can lose a case in a heartbeat, but cultivating a professional attitude and sticking to the facts will make you not only a lawyer respected by both the judge and opposing counsel, but an advocate whose arguments carry the force necessary to do a client's case justice.

Part II

Writing Well

Chapter 8

The Role of Writing in the Legal System

WORDS ARE THE HEART OF the legal system. Obviously, it is impossible to question witnesses or create arguments without the use of language. The written word is the basis of laws and statutes and, thus, it determines our future and history. Without words and writing, a lawyer would be immobilized. When a lawyer chooses words carelessly, an argument may be misinterpreted or a small mistake may cause the entire case to be lost.

IN THIS CHAPTER	
• **Uses for Writing in Legal Practice** ◦ Formal Writing ◦ Informal Writing • **Ramifications of Legal Writing** ◦ Ambiguity Leads to Controversy ◦ Citation of Sources • **Shift in Function and Presentation**	◦ Legal Writing in the Public Sphere ◦ Moving Away from Legalese • **Use of Modern Technologies** ◦ E-mail ◦ Videoconferencing ◦ Online Research • **Summation**

USES FOR WRITING IN LEGAL PRACTICE

The stereotypical TV lawyer spends all of his or her time presenting verbal arguments in a courtroom. However, lawyers must also communicate a great deal via writing. A lawyer must communicate the detailed facts and legal rules associated with a case, along with the outcome being advocated. The recipient of this information (a client, supervisor, fellow lawyer, judge, or law clerk) should not be expected to sit through a lengthy, complex oral explanation. For this reason, lawyers explain such things in a letter, memorandum, or court brief.

Legal writing can serve a functional, informational, or persuasive role. A will or contract, for example, is a functional document. It does not have to be persuasive or entertaining, but it must be accurate, complete, and comprehensible. Other types of legal writing—such as memoranda, letters to clients, and statements of facts in briefs—serve an informational purpose: to objectively convey facts and developments or to provide a balanced analysis of some issue. This category of writing can be formal or informal, depending on the situation and the recipient. Finally, some legal writing is aimed at persuading the reader to agree with a given point of view. Persuasive writing (used, for example, in appellate briefs or in negotiation letters written on a client's behalf) must be more engaging compared with the other types.

Formal Writing

Formal writing requires planning, organizing, and revision. One must also take care to maintain a formal tone. For example, formal writing should not make use of personal information, first- or second-person voice (the pronouns "I," "we," "you," "me," etc.), colloquialisms (for example, use "children" rather than "kids"), clichés, or contractions. (More details on how to achieve a formal tone are included in Chapter 10.) Most documents that are intended to leave the legal office should be written using a formal tone and style. These include contracts, wills, affidavits, pleadings in litigation matters, and written opinions on cases. Often, lawyers must also write formal letters to clients or on a client's behalf.

Informal Writing

When you are writing informally, it is still important to follow basic grammar rules, use complete sentences, and check spelling. The tone of such writing, however, is clearly more casual and conversational. Informal writing is common in inter-office memoranda, business transactions, and e-mail.

RAMIFICATIONS OF LEGAL WRITING

Accuracy and comprehensibility are the most important concerns in legal writing. Clients, judges, administrators, and others rely on information and opinions from lawyers. These people must be able to trust the lawyer to give them the facts. Of course, it is essential to be clear and accurate in reporting overall legal conclusions, but it is just as important to ensure the details are correct—names, dates, addresses, and dollar amounts. Even small mistakes in your writing will negatively affect a reader's perception of you and cast doubt on your abilities.

Inaccuracies not only damage a lawyer's credibility, but they can also have legal ramifications. Simple mistakes, such as using the wrong word, omitting a fact, or inserting something somewhere it does not belong, can have seriously detrimental consequences. The worst of these consequences is being sued for malpractice by one's own client.

Ambiguity Leads to Controversy

In the courtroom, words from legal documents are debated and used as rationales. If your writing is not clear and precise, it may be used by others in ways that you did not intend. For instance, courtroom debates regarding same-sex marriage generally center on the definition of marriage. Recently, this issue has been argued in the California Supreme Court. This same California court passed a decision in 1948, *Perez v. Sharp*, legalizing interracial marriages. According to the *Perez* decision, "The essence of the right to marry is freedom to join in marriage with the person of one's choice."

The writers of this decision likely intended this statement to refer only to the marriage of people of different races. But now, several decades later, these words are being used to defend same-sex marriages. The state of California, having declared sixty years ago that there is no valid ground for making distinctions on whom one can or cannot marry, created a potentially unintended ambiguity that is driving current legal decisions. As a result, the supreme court overturned two marriage laws, making same-sex marriage legal in that state in May 2008.

Other legal texts, such as the Digital Millennium Copyright Act and even the U.S. Constitution, have left (sometimes intentionally) much ambiguity and have often become sources of major controversy. The Second Amendment is one example. What exactly does "the right to keep and bear Arms" mean? What does a militia look like today? Of course, the writers of the Constitution could not have anticipated every possibility that could arise in the future. However, ambiguities in their writing continue to generate questions and debates years later. In your own writing, you should strive for clarity, always giving explicit definitions and explanations of your intended point.

Citation of Sources

Another legal concern in reference to writing is citation. It is acceptable to borrow words and ideas from other writings; in fact, this can add credibility to your writing. For instance, when you discuss what the law is or what it should be, it is important to cite authorities. This makes your readers more likely to trust what you have to say. Just remember to cite the source of the information. Of course, if you use a direct quotation (another person's word-for-word statement enclosed in quotation marks), you must cite the source of that quote. However, any time you take ideas from another source (even if not in the form of a direct quotation), a citation is necessary. See Chapter 14 for more on legal citations.

SHIFT IN FUNCTION AND PRESENTATION

Just as most things in our world have changed and evolved, so has legal writing. It has become more common to find bits of legal writing entering the public sphere, and the tone of legal writing is shifting to include more "plain English."

Legal Writing in the Public Sphere

Legal writing is not used exclusively by legal practitioners; it has permeated the public sphere. Legal warnings appear on many common items, such as DVDs, fast-food coffee cups, websites, and other products. For example, on the back of the DVD case for the movie *Little Miss Sunshine*, a statement reads:

> The unauthorized reproduction or distribution of this copyrighted work is illegal. Criminal copyright infringement, including infringement without monetary gain, is investigated by the FBI and is punishable by up to 5 years in federal prison and a fine of $250,000.

Not only does the public see, read, and hear many legal warnings when they watch movies or buy a cup of coffee, but they also have access to larger bodies of legal writing. Many lawyers, law professors, and other legal professionals now have blogs where they point out the intricacies of issues and cases, explain legal theory, or give their opinions. Beyond that, the Internet and public libraries have made legal texts more accessible to the general public. Any person who would like to read the details of a case will most likely be able to locate the information online.

Moving Away from Legalese

The incorporation of legal writing into the public sphere has gone hand in hand with the move away from legalese. "Legalese" refers to legal language that is inaccessible to laypeople. It is essentially a specialized vernacular used in the legal profession. Legalese uses long sentences, Latin terms, and a wide vocabulary; it is abstract and shows regard for the average person's need to understand. Legal writing is notorious for being wordy, convoluted, and largely incomprehensible.

This type of writing does not give the untrained reader a fair chance of grasping and dealing with the core issues of a case. Instead, the core issues are often buried and distorted by excessive wordiness. In recent years, the Plain Language Movement has emerged to promote writing (in law, academia, government, and business) that is clear and understandable to the public. The Plain Language Movement opposes writing that lends power and authority to its writer (through the use of long sentences, jargon, and a high degree of formality) at the expense of the reader. It is hoped that such reforms will allow the public to better comprehend important legal documents, such as contracts and laws. It is thought that the use of plain language will lead to clearer and more effective communication. This movement away from highly formal, specialized, and ritualistic language marks a significant change in legal writing.

Plain English advocates ask: why use five words when you can effectively say the same thing using one? Modern teachers of legal writing suggest that wordiness and unnecessary phrases (such as "it is determined that," "it is apparent that," and "it should be noted that") be omitted. Legalese attempts to thoroughly cover all possibilities. Plain English, on the other hand, holds that legal writing should cover all reasonably expected possibilities, and that it is impractical to cover every possibility imaginable. The basic idea is that a balance must be achieved between thoroughness and conciseness. (Conciseness is discussed in more detail in Chapter 10.) Word choices can also enhance clarity; for instance, you may say "stop" instead of "cease and desist," "explain" or "clarify" instead of "elucidate," and "immediately" instead of "forthwith."

None of this is to suggest that legal writing cannot be complex. Matters of the law are encircled by complexities! Good legal writing, however, takes the complexities and explains them in a simple, comprehensible way. It is necessary to write with your intended audience in mind, although you do not want to sound patronizing or to leave out complex details. The goal is to gain enough knowledge of a legal topic that you could explain it to any given audience.

Of course, there will be times when legalese is allowable or even necessary, but this language should still be used with the audience and situation in mind. There are certainly times when ritualistic or ceremonial language is appropriate, and in those cases, the ceremonial language should be used. It is also often necessary to strike a balance between the use of common language and legalese.

USE OF MODERN TECHNOLOGIES

The evolution of modern technologies has affected the legal writing process. Computers allow writers to quickly and easily store, copy, and send documents. In these and other ways, technology adds convenience to a lawyer's life. This convenience is sometimes entangled with additional concerns and complications, however.

E-mail

E-mail is a valuable tool for lawyers today, but it must be used with care and discretion. A 2007 American Bar Association report found that

97 percent of attorneys use e-mail for regular work correspondence. More than 70 percent of those respondents use e-mail even for case status reports and memoranda/briefs. Other e-mail applications include client billing, marketing, and court filing. Obviously, e-mail can facilitate instantaneous communication and can be much quicker and easier than sending a letter or making a phone call. However, because of the informal tone of many e-mails, a lawyer can become too comfortable in e-mail interactions. It is important to remember that if you were to say the wrong thing in an e-mail, unintended consequence including a malpractice suit could follow. Even in e-mail correspondence, it is necessary to choose your words wisely. Below are several tips for professional e-mail usage.

- Separate your work and home/personal e-mails. It is easiest to keep two separate accounts.
- An e-mail address that uses your name or the name of your firm looks most professional.
- Whenever possible, avoid free e-mail providers (such as gmail, yahoo, or hotmail). These providers are fine for personal use, but can appear unprofessional in a work context. Instead, consider using your own domain name (for example, john.bartlett@smithlaw.com). If your firm does not have a domain name, you can get one easily and inexpensively at a site such as GoDaddy.com.
- Respond to e-mails quickly, within twenty-four hours. Even if you don't have a clear answer, it is best to respond and say, "I am looking into this. I will have a more thorough answer in the next week." If you are planning to be out of the office, schedule an automated reply.
- Keep records of all correspondence.
- When sending an e-mail to a group of people who do not know one another, consider putting the e-mail addresses in the "Bcc" field. This ensures that recipients will not be able to see one another's e-mail addresses. Many people prefer this because they consider one's e-mail address to be private information.

- Don't get so casual that you forget the basics of letter writing. Make sure to always include a salutation and a closing as well as your name.
- Follow basic grammar and punctuation rules.
- Check with clients to make sure they received and were able to open any attachments.

Videoconferencing

Videoconferencing is popular within the legal profession. This technology allows lawyers to discuss cases, question witnesses, seek counsel from outside experts, hold meetings with clients or partners, and conduct interviews from afar. Via video, lawyers are also able to facilitate professional development and training and to share or edit legal documents. Videoconferencing provides the illusion of face-to-face communication when involved parties are geographically distant from one another. These capabilities certainly save time and travel expense. They also further blur the lines between formal prose and everyday speech. Rather than communicating via the postal system using formally written documents, lawyers communicate with their clients and others using plain spoken English.

Even some criminal trials have been held via videoconference (when the legal professionals are in a different location from the witness, who may be testifying from prison). Again, this saves time and travel expense while also negating any security concerns with prisoners. Many questions have been raised regarding the fairness of this trial method, however. For example, can the credibility of a witness be accurately assessed via video, and can jurors fairly judge a defendant when his or her presence is merely a televised image? These trials have further implications for the lawyer who is representing the defendant. That attorney has to choose between being in the courtroom and being in the prison with the client.

Videoconferencing certainly raises some concerns when used in criminal trials, but it is undoubtedly a useful tool, allowing interactions that were not previously possible by enabling lawyers to overcome geographic and logistical constraints.

Online Research

In many cases, it is now possible for lawyers to complete their research without entering a law library. Online services, such as the Westlaw and

Lexis databases and the Internet, are available to aid in legal research. The services of Westlaw and Lexis are preferred over the Internet, although the Internet can be used with caution. Databases such as Westlaw and Lexis can be expensive to use, but with a high price come high expectations of quality materials. The information found through these services is trusted, reliable, and up to date. The Internet, on the other hand, is free, but the information available there is not always reliable. Few Internet legal research sites have been peer-reviewed by practicing lawyers. Further, there is no guarantee that any information found online is up to date.

The Internet may be used:

- To locate factual background information.
- To find a specific item, such as a specific case that you know the name of.
- To confirm what you are already reasonably certain of.
- When it doesn't matter what you find, and you just need an example.

The Internet should not be used:

- To locate, interpret, and confirm applicable laws for the purpose of coming up with legal advice.
- When you are in a hurry and need quick answers. Research on the Internet takes longer than other forms of research because you generally need to find a number of websites and cross-check the information for accuracy.

SUMMATION

Words—both written and spoken—are essential to the practice of law. Lawyers use the written word to create contracts, prepare briefs, send e-mail messages, and more. The ways in which words are used have changed over time, with a move away from legalese and the incorporation of more informal communication channels such as e-mail and videoconferencing. Regardless of the situation, care must always be taken to avoid ambiguity and the serious complications that can arise from even small mistakes or oversights.

Chapter 9

Organization: Form and Logic

PROPER ORGANIZATION OF WRITING ELIMINATES clutter and confusion. If ideas are simply thrown out, the result will be difficult for readers to follow. Readers will end up confused and frustrated as they try to sort through the clutter trying to identify the logical flow of ideas. Some writers jump from one idea to the next without giving readers any signal of what is to come. Ideas then become jumbled and the overall message is unclear. You must separate and organize your ideas to ensure clarity in writing.

IN THIS CHAPTER	

• **Organizing Sentences**
• **Organizing Paragraphs, Sections, and Entire Documents**
  ○ Paragraph Structure
  ○ Document Structure
• **Transitions**
	• **Page Layout**
	  ○ Small Segments
	  ○ Aesthetically Pleasing Content
	• **Coherence and Logic**
	  ○ Promoting Coherence
	  ○ Maintaining Logic
	• **Summation**

ORGANIZING SENTENCES

Sentences can be organized in a variety of ways. First of all, a sentence is a complete, independent clause, consisting of a subject and a predicate. Both independent and dependent clauses have a subject and a verb. However, independent clauses can stand alone, whereas a dependent clause requires another clause to complete its meaning. When constructing a sentence, be sure to avoid fragments and run-ons. A sentence fragment is a phrase or a dependent clause that cannot stand alone as a complete sentence but is presented as one. A run-on sentence consists of two independent clauses that are improperly joined. (For information on how to correctly join independent clauses, see Chapter 12.)

- **Correct:** The debriefings lasted several hundred hours, during which time Ms. Vandaveer provided information on a number of subjects.
- **Fragment (Incorrect):** During which time Ms. Vandaveer provided information on a number of subjects.
- **Run-on (Incorrect):** The debriefings lasted several hundred hours, Ms. Vandaveer provided information on a number of subjects.

Sentences can be categorized into four types as described below. In addition to these types, sentences can be classified as either periodic or cumulative. Periodic sentences begin with a modifying phrase or clause and end with an independent clause. Cumulative sentences are the opposite: they begin with an independent clause and end with a modifying construction. In your writing, use the sentence type that works best in each specific context and try to add variety. Readers will get bored if all of your sentences are structured the same way.

- **Simple** (one independent clause): The plaintiff argued his case adamantly.
- **Compound** (more than one independent clause): Mr. and Mrs. Prunty were very upset about the burglary, but they decided not to press charges.
- **Complex** (one independent clause and at least one dependent clause): Although the defendant had some misgivings, the trial was held via videoconference.
- **Compound-Complex** (more than one independent clause and at least one dependent clause): Although it was a clear violation of his constitutional rights, Casey Devanhart was given a life sentence, and he has not been allowed to contest it.

ORGANIZING PARAGRAPHS, SECTIONS, AND ENTIRE DOCUMENTS

It is necessary to organize the information you present in a manner that makes it clear and easy to follow. Written material should not jump randomly from one point to another; rather, ideas should flow logically or sequentially. Good organization will help to ensure that your readers grasp your intended meaning.

Paragraph Structure

Each paragraph should be structured with an introduction, a body, and a conclusion.

- **Introduction:** Each paragraph should have a topic sentence (generally the first sentence) that introduces the basic subject of the paragraph. This topic sentence should include broad, general ideas and not many details.
- **Body:** The body of the paragraph contains information that expands upon, explains, and provides support for

the topic sentence. The body contains the details and makes up the bulk of the paragraph.

- **Conclusion:** Each paragraph should have a concluding sentence that summarizes the ideas covered in the paragraph, concisely states the consequence or conclusion, and provides a smooth transition into the next paragraph. This sentence is in some ways similar to, but should not repeat, the introductory topic sentence.

Document Structure

There are a variety of ways in which the information can be organized within a given document. Each organizational approach has its advantages and disadvantages. It is important to determine the document's purpose and then decide which organizational approach will work best to meet the specific goals of the document. The most important thing is to make a clear determination regarding the organization style to use and stick to that pattern for the entirety of the document. A few organizational patterns are listed below.

- **General to specific.** This method of organization begins with a general statement and then presents specific details related to the original statement. For example, a document may begin by stating the overall outcome of a case and then proceed to give the specific details and reasoning that led to that conclusion. Often, the conclusion is what readers are most interested in. It can be helpful to present the conclusion at the beginning of the document so that readers who are pressed for time can quickly and easily locate the most important information.
- **Specific to general.** This pattern is the reverse of that above: it begins with the most specific information and progresses to overarching general statements. A document using this organizational approach may begin by describing the specific details and reasoning of a case and end by stating the overall conclusion. This style of writing is more apt to leave the reader in suspense, waiting to learn the outcome. Although suspense is generally not

the goal of legal writing, there are times when it is appropriate to organize documents in this way.

- **IMRAD.** This is a pattern of organization used frequently in scientific writing. IMRAD is an acronym that stands for *introduction, methods, results, and discussion.* This refers to the sections of a research paper and the order in which they should appear.
  - **Introduction.** The introduction should move from general to specific, supply background information, and identify the research question.
  - **Methods.** In the methods section, the design of the study is explained and details are given about exactly what the researcher did.
  - **Results.** The results section presents the outcome of the research, often using tables and graphs. It does not include a comment on the results, but only presents them objectively.
  - **Discussion.** The discussion section comments on the results, giving a brief summary of the main findings and how they relate to the initial research question. This section also addresses limitations of the study, points out relationships between the study and other research, and identifies further research needed. The discussion is typically organized in a manner opposite that used for the introduction, moving from specific to general.
- **TREAT.** This format is recommended for writing that analyzes a legal issue and reports a lawyer's conclusions. TREAT is a revised version of IRAC, a form of writing taught in many legal writing courses. TREAT is an acronym for *thesis, rule, explanation, application, thesis restated.* Again, this refers to the sections of a document and the order in which those sections should appear.
  - **Thesis.** A thesis is generally one sentence long and briefly specifies the basic issue and the writer's position on the issue. Using this organizational approach, the writer begins by stating his or her position on the issue at hand.

- **Rule.** In the second section of the TREAT format, the rule of law is discussed. A rule states the legal principles and requirements that preside over a legal issue. Any given legal issue is governed by a rule or multiple rules.
- **Explanation.** The explanation section cites legal authorities and explains how the rule has operated in various situations. This section explains how the rule should generally be interpreted or applied.
- **Application.** In the application section, the rule is applied to the case at hand, and an explanation is provided on how the rule relates to the client's facts and how it will operate in this specific instance.
- **Thesis.** The final portion of the document returns to and restates the original thesis.

TRANSITIONS

A transition is a word or phrase that helps a document to flow smoothly by emphasizing the connections between one idea and the next. A few examples of transitional words and phrases are listed below. These transitions can appear at the beginning or in the middle of sentences.

- *Also, furthermore, moreover, similarly, thus, consequently, especially, finally*
- *In addition, as a result, for the most part, for example, first of all, after all, in the long run*

Transitions are also used between paragraphs or sections to seamlessly connect the ideas represented in these larger components of a document. As discussed earlier, each paragraph should have an introductory sentence and a concluding sentence. Often, these sentences serve as transitions by indicating the relationship of the given paragraph to previous paragraphs or to the overall document as a whole. Transitional words, phrases, and sentences allow a document to move from one idea to the next without the shift seeming abrupt.

PAGE LAYOUT

Another consideration for writers is how a document appears on the page. Does the document look accessible, or might a reader find it intimidating? Differences in page layout can affect a reader's perception of the text. Readers will likely overlook or avoid information that, upon first glance, appears too complex, and the arrangement of items on the page can contribute to the apparent complexity.

Small Segments

Be wary of paragraphs, sections, and entire documents that are too long. Smaller blocks of text are perceived as more manageable and less daunting to readers, while long sequences may seem dense and forbidding. Readers can also get through short segments somewhat quickly, helping you to limit the risk of reader apathy or distraction. Short, clearly labeled sections promote easy, straightforward reading and enhance content organization.

With paragraphs, short should not mean superficial. Even short paragraphs should offer important information and insights. The primary thing to remember is that each paragraph should have one specific focus. Often, paragraphs grow too long because they lose focus and attempt to cover multiple topics. If a paragraph contains more than one idea, it should be broken into multiple paragraphs—one for each idea. Even focused paragraphs can become too long, in which case they should also be broken into multiple smaller paragraphs. The ideal is for all paragraphs to be roughly the same length, leading to continuity within a document. Although smaller paragraphs are preferred, it is possible to create paragraphs that are too short and that make the text seem choppy or abrupt. Use good judgment to help you create a document that is accessible and easy to read.

Aesthetically Pleasing Content

It is important for a document to look uncluttered, aesthetically pleasing, and laid out clearly in terms of organization of content. Again, the appearance of a page—including the use of numbered or bulleted lists, sufficient white space, and avoidance of unnecessary graphical elements—can favorably influence the reader's perception of the overall text.

- **Numbered or bulleted lists.** Numbers and bullets aid in creating text that is both well organized and easy to read.

Numbered or bulleted lists can break up a dense block of text and present key points in a way that does not seem forced and artificial. These lists also display information in a format that is logical and immediately interpretable, obviating the need to search paragraphs for desired information. In general, bullets are preferred over numbers. Numbers should be used only when there is a specific need for text references to items (by number) or when the items make up a particular sequence. For example, use numbers for a list of steps or a nonsequential group requiring identifiers ("see profile 3 above"). Following are some tips for using numbered or bulleted lists.

- Explain the nature or purpose of the list in the text that precedes the list.
- Simple bullets are best. Basic dots or boxes are generally preferred over arrows or check marks.
- Don't allow list items to get too long. Shorter is better. Ideally, a bulleted or numbered item should take up less than three lines of type.
- When bulleted items have to be long, add inline headers (such as the ones leading off the primary entries in this list).
- Within a list, follow some sort of organizational pattern, such as chronological order. When there is no such pattern that can be followed, place the most important information at the beginning.
- Don't create too many sublevels using indentation. Indentation is useful for organizing information and indicating hierarchy. However, it can become confusing when complex orderings of items are used. When more than three levels of indentation are needed, consider arranging the information in some other fashion (as in a table).
- Be consistent in the use of punctuation and capitalization in lists.

- **White space.** It is important to leave white space in your documents (space that is occupied neither by words nor by graphical elements). Retaining some white space adds visual appeal to a page by making it look less cluttered, as well as more organized and approachable. Following are suggestions for using white space in your documents.

  - Use margins (typically one inch) at the top, bottom, and sides of a page.
  - Leave space between sections; generally, extra space is left before and after headings and in some cases even between paragraphs.

- **Uncluttered pages.** Some graphical elements (such as tables) can be useful for presenting complex information. However, they can be overused, taking up unnecessary space and making a page seem congested. As previously mentioned, cluttered pages are intimidating and confusing to readers. Use graphical elements only when they are necessary, and strive to keep pages free of congestion.
  - Borders, shaded backgrounds, and horizontal or vertical lines should generally be avoided.
  - The use of a variety of fonts can have a cluttering effect. Fonts should be limited in number and used consistently throughout the entire document. If the color, size, or density of a font is to be changed, it must be done strategically and consistently.
  - Graphical text enhancements (such as superscripts, subscripts, strike-through, shadowing, embossing, and texturing) should generally be avoided. They are distracting and look unprofessional. In particular, it is not a good idea to write in all capital letters (to show emphasis, for example).

COHERENCE AND LOGIC

As has been a recurring theme in this chapter, writing should be coherent and logical. All ideas should fit together and be interrelated, and the document should be easy to follow. Successful writing is clear and concise, and promotes ease of reading.

Promoting Coherence

To prevent reader confusion, some repetition in writing is useful. Of course, you do not want your writing to become redundant and boring, but within limits, repetition can be positive. For example, in referring to a concept or object, it is best to use the same term every time. You may also use close synonyms, but don't change terms haphazardly. Always make sure that it will be clear to your readers what concept or object you are referring to.

- **Clear:** I name Myra Berg as *personal representative* of this will. No *personal representative* of this will shall be required to furnish bond or other security as *personal representative.* If the above-named person is unable or unwilling to serve as *personal representative,* then I name Kami Brown to serve in that capacity.
- **Unclear:** I name Myra Berg as *personal representative* of this will. No *administrator* of this will shall be required to furnish bond or other security as *personal representative.* If the above-named person is unable or unwilling to serve as *administrator,* then I name Kami Brown to serve in that capacity.

Another way in which repetition can be useful is in a standardized sentence structure. As mentioned earlier in this chapter, it is best to vary sentence structure. However, intentionally repeating a sentence structure can at times improve clarity and strengthen emphasis.

- Whereas, Landlord is the fee owner of certain real property being, lying, and situated in Fulton County, Illinois, such read property having a street address of 549 South Bend Road, Cuba, IL 65401.

  Whereas, Landlord desires to lease the Premises to Tenant upon the terms and conditions as contained herein, and

  Whereas, Tenant desires to lease the Premises from Landlord on the terms and conditions as contained herein. . . .

Coherence is also promoted by adherence to basic grammar and punctuation rules. These topics are discussed in Chapters 11 and 12 of this book. *The Chicago Manual of Style* as well as the MLA (Modern Language Association) and APA (American Psychological Association) handbooks are also great resources.

Maintaining Logic

It is important to keep sight of the big picture and structure your information in ways that make sense. Sections, paragraphs, and even sentences should be divided where breaks between ideas logically occur. As mentioned previously, each paragraph—and, similarly, each section and each sentence—should be devoted to one central idea. If paragraphs, sections, or sentences become too long, you are probably trying to cover too many ideas.

The use of parallel construction is another way to help readers through the use of logical thought processes. An example of parallel construction is the use of consistent structural wording in a list of items.

- **Correct:** The plaintiff described her day: she had eaten breakfast, gone swimming, met with an independent contractor at 11 a.m., and washed her car before noon.
- **Incorrect:** The plaintiff described her day: she had eaten breakfast, gone swimming, then to an independent contractor meeting at 11 a.m., and to the car wash before noon.

SUMMATION

Organization takes time, patience, and planning. You may have to make multiple revisions before producing a text that flows smoothly from one idea to the next. Scattered ideas and lack of order in writing can be daunting, prompting the reader to wonder, "Where do I start?" Don't allow your writing to become cluttered and unapproachable. Take deliberate measures to ensure that the documents you produce are accessible and easy to follow. Your readers will surely appreciate it.

Chapter 10

Style: Clarity, Conciseness, and Voice

A **WRITER'S MESSAGE MUST ALWAYS** be clear and straightforward, never cluttered with unnecessary information or extra words. The most important points of any document should be obvious and unmistakable. These messages should also be presented with an authoritative voice, imparting credibility to the writer and influencing readers to agree with the arguments. Effective writing conveys messages in ways that are clear and compelling.

IN THIS CHAPTER	

• **Audience and Situational Analysis**
• **Clarity**
  ◦ Parts of an Argument
• **Conciseness**
  ◦ Omitting Needless Words, Phrases, and Sentences
	◦ Using Outlines
	◦ Rereading Aloud
	• **Voice**
	  ◦ Formal Writing
	  ◦ Writing Matter-of-Factly
	• **Summation**

AUDIENCE AND SITUATIONAL ANALYSIS

An important part of successful writing is analyzing the intended audience and the situation. Different writing strategies should be employed at different times based on the purpose of the writing. Some audiences will be more familiar with the information than others and will therefore need fewer details. The tone of writing should change depending on the situation and the audience. Some situations require more friendliness whereas others call for greater distance. To some audiences, the writer is an authority; to other audiences, he or she is a colleague of equal or lesser status. Whatever the case, written texts should always be appropriate to the audience and situation. The goal is to write in ways that will be clear and easily interpreted by your target audience. Keep the following steps in mind as you write.

- Identify the target audience. Consider demographics such as age range, education level, profession, culture, and language. These and other factors will influence how a person interprets your message.
- Identify the needs of the target audience. For example, what information do they need to know? How will they use this information? How much do they know already?
- Determine what you, as the writer, can do to address and meet the audience's needs.

CLARITY

In face-to-face communication, a speaker can usually judge how well the audience understands the message being delivered. When the audience is one person, that person may give audible cues (such as "oh" or "uh huh"), nod his or her head, appear confused, or respond with other nonverbal signals to indicate his or her level of comprehension. The speaker can also stop and ask questions to ensure that the audience is grasping the intended meaning. As long as the speaker feels confident that the audience is getting the message, he or she can continue. On the other hand, when confusion is apparent, the speaker can pause to clarify.

Of course, written communication does not enjoy these advantages. It does not share the responsiveness possible with face-to-face communication. The writer is typically not present when the text is being read, and he or she usually never gets the chance to clear up any misunderstandings. Also keep in mind that written texts aren't subject to the temporal limitations of the spoken word. Many historical and religious texts that were written thousands of years ago are still widely read or discussed today. Even the U.S. Constitution is more than 200 years old. For these reasons, clear writing is essential. Your written documents may live well beyond you. You likely will not be present to respond to the reactions of your readers and clarify any misunderstanding or confusion. Thus, it is essential that any document you draft be unquestionably clear.

Many organizational, style, and writing techniques are available to help make your text more clear. Various techniques are discussed throughout this book. For example, Chapter 9 covers organization, transitions, and page layout, which all contribute to clarity in writing. Chapters 11 and 12 discuss how to use grammar and punctuation in ways that promote clarity.

Parts of an Argument

Clarity can also be enhanced by paying attention to the logical elements listed below. These elements represent the core of a writer's message and are important in making that message clear to readers.

Thesis

A thesis is a short, usually one- or two-sentence statement that succinctly describes the purpose of the document and perhaps previews the main ideas. A thesis reveals what the writer intends to establish. The thesis statement generally appears at the end of the opening or introductory paragraph and serves to make the primary message of the document clear to readers. A good thesis statement is:

- An assertion that constitutes an active stance, rather than a factual statement or observation or the announcement of a topic. It should propose an idea with which someone could reasonably disagree.

  - **Assertion:** This case centers on junior high school boy who committed suicide in May of 2008 as a consequence of the abusive relationship initiated by his step-father.
  - **Factual statement:** This case relates to junior high school boy who committed suicide in May of 2008.
- Specific and focused, rather than vague or general. Thesis statements should avoid imprecise language (such as "it seems that").
  - **Specific:** Because approximately 50 million Americans are without health care, the U.S. government should implement a nationwide health care plan.
  - **Vague:** The U.S. government appears to be shirking its responsibility to do something about the health care crisis.
- Centered on one point: the main idea of the document. Offering several main points impedes the goal of clarity.
  - **Focused:** Taylor Brown is entitled to the sum of $100,000 to compensate for psychological damages caused by her ex-husband.
  - **Less focused:** Taylor Brown is entitled to the sum of $100,000 to compensate for psychological damages caused by her ex-husband; her physical losses are also notable, but are less important to her than the psychological ones.
- A matter-of-fact statement that does not use the first person. For instance, thesis statements should not include the phrase "I believe" or "in my opinion."
  - **Correct:** Because more than 70 percent of Americans are dissatisfied with government spending, U.S. tax dollars should be reallocated: more money should be spent solving world hunger and less money should be spent fighting the War on Terror.
  - **Incorrect:** I believe world hunger is more important than the War on Terror, and U.S. government spending should be reevaluated accordingly.

Qualifiers

Qualifiers are statements that oppose or question a document's thesis. It is always beneficial to address opposing views. This will clarify your stance—making it clear what you believe and also what you do not believe. Including qualifiers will also enhance your credibility by showing that you are not afraid to acknowledge opposing arguments.

Rebuttals

Rebuttals are responses to the qualifiers, answers to assertions that oppose or question the writer's message. Providing clear responses to opposing points of view will ultimately make the writer's argument stronger and will also address many of the concerns or questions that readers may have.

Conclusion

At the end of any document, it is important to again make the thesis or primary message clear and to demonstrate that it has emerged victorious over the qualifiers.

CONCISENESS

Lawyers are not known for being concise. In fact, their writing is notorious for being wordy, aloof, and superfluous. As mentioned in Chapter 8, however, with the move away from legalese, lawyers are now encouraged to be more direct. In your writing, do not mimic the traditional law documents you have read and studied. Instead, strive for conciseness.

Concise writing conveys a plethora of ideas using few words; it is succinct. It leaves out superfluous details and makes the important messages unmistakable. Deliberate steps must be taken to achieve conciseness in writing.

Omitting Needless Words, Phrases, and Sentences

There is no need to clutter your writing with unnecessary information. Each sentence should be examined carefully for extraneous words or phrases, and each paragraph should be scrutinized for excess sentences. Every word and idea should serve a purpose.

Many common expressions impede the objective of conciseness.

- Use "because" instead of "the reason why is that."
- Use "hastily" instead of "in a hasty manner."
- Say "the plaintiff is persistent" rather than "the plaintiff is a persistent one."
- "The fact that" is always unnecessary and should be avoided.
  - Use "though" or "although" instead of "in spite of the fact that."
  - Say "his bad luck" instead of "the fact that he had bad luck."
- Phrases such as "who is" and "which was" are often superfluous.
  - Say "his friend, a major executive in the company" instead of "his friend, who is a major executive in the company."
  - Say "that case, the hardest one I ever dealt with" instead of "that case, which was the hardest one I ever dealt with."

Sometimes expressing a succession of related ideas using several short sentences is less effective than combining those ideas into one longer but more concise statement.

- **More concise:** Her brother is one of the suspects in a murder that took place during a party at her house on August 24. (22 words)
- **Less concise:** The murder took place at her house on August 24. There was a party going on at her house when it happened. Her brother is one of the suspects. (29 words)

Sentences written in active voice tend to be more concise than those written in passive voice.

- **Active:** Both of them will always regret that day.
- **Passive:** That day will always be regretted by both of them.

Sentences written in the positive form tend to be more concise than those written in the negative form.

- **Positive:** The defendant ignored my request for more information.
- **Negative:** The defendant did not pay any attention to my request for more information.

Using Outlines

It is helpful to create an outline before you begin to write. This will ensure that important parts of the message are included in the document and that unnecessary information is left out of the document. An outline allows a writer to get an overall view of the subject and provides the writer with a plan. Following this plan will enhance conciseness by helping the writer focus on what's important and ignore what is not. A writer who does not use an outline is likely to lack clear focus and may end up rambling.

When you create an outline, remember to consider the target audience. Some audiences will need to know more information than others. A message to a colleague who had worked alongside you on a case would include significantly fewer details than one directed at a potential witness who knew little or nothing about the case. There are several different ways to approach outlines.

- **Logical outline.** A writer may start simply by writing his or her message in three broad sentences. These sentences will likely correspond to the thesis, qualifiers, and conclusion.
- **Stylistic outline.** A writer may preface the outline with introductory remarks and end it with concluding remarks, thus setting the stage at the beginning and drawing the curtain at the end.
- **Detailed outline.** A writer may expand upon some or all simple-sentence main points in an outline by adding simple-sentence subpoints. Each subpoint should give details that elaborate on the meaning of the main point it is meant to support. In a detailed outline, a main point is expanded upon to the highest level of detail possible.

Rereading Aloud

Once the draft of a written document is completed, it helps to read the document aloud. Writers are more likely to recognize errors such as repetition, awkward phrasing, or transitional gaps when they hear a text read aloud. Hearing the text may also help identify unnecessary words and phrases. This proofreading method forces a writer to concentrate on the content of the document and helps ensure that the message is presented effectively. There are two main things to focus on when rereading a text aloud.

- **Content.** How does each statement or idea contribute to conveying the overall message? If a statement or an idea does not contribute to the main message, it should be deleted.
- **Presentation.** Listen carefully for errors in pronunciation and wording.

VOICE

Voice refers to how writing "sounds" on the page. Voice is one's style of writing—the tone a writer uses, the words he or she chooses, the way he or she arranges sentences. Established writers each have their own voice, and each creates texts that sound unique in some way. Like handwriting, an individual's written voice is often recognizable, representing a distinct style. Good writers allow their voices to shine through despite the circumstances under which they are writing. Note the difference in voice between the following passages. The first is informal and satirical, whereas the second is formal and professional.

- **Take a lesson from the Chinese.** We need to build a 2000-mile long wall along our southern border. This will have two benefits. First of all, when I'm worried I like to stay busy. Building a giant wall is a great way to keep the nation's mind off how many immigrants enter the country through airports. Second, this wall might actually keep people out. If it's built *right,* not like that picket fence the Russians threw up across Berlin. (From Stephen Colbert's *I Am America (and So Can You!)*)

- The respondents, Michelle Thomas and her immediate family, applied for asylum. They checked boxes on the application form that indicated their claim rested upon fear of persecution in their native South Africa because of (1) their "political opinion[s]," and (2) their "membership in a particular social group." In proceedings before the Immigration Judge, they emphasized their fear of persecution because of their race (they are white) and their kinship with Michelle's father-in-law, "Boss Ronnie," a white South African who allegedly held racist views and mistreated black workers at the company at which he was a foreman. The Immigration Judge, focusing upon questions of race and political views, rejected their claim. (From *Gonzales v. Thomas,* 547 U.S. (2006))

Formal Writing

Keep in mind that your voice will vary depending on your target audience. In a memo to a colleague, for example, an authoritative voice may be interpreted as condescending. In most legal writing, however, it is important to maintain a voice of authority and reliability. In part, such an authoritative voice can be achieved with the use of formal tone, which was discussed briefly in Chapter 8. Also remember from Chapter 8 that legal writing is shifting from the use of legalese to the use of plain English. This will certainly affect the voice of legal writers, making them seem less aloof and distant. It is important to balance the use of common language with some degree of formality, however. Suggestions for formality in writing follow.

- Avoid slang and colloquial terms.
  - **Correct:** She was intoxicated on the night of the accident.
  - **Incorrect:** She was plastered on the night of the accident.
- Whenever possible, avoid slash constructions, such as *and/or* or *professor/researcher.*
- Refrain from using contractions, such as *haven't* and *shouldn't.*

- When possible, avoid using symbols (&, @, #). Use symbols only when they are an established part of a statute, company name, or e-mail address. It is also acceptable to use the dollar sign when citing monetary amounts.
    - For even-dollar amounts, it is acceptable to write either "two hundred dollars" or "$200." Do not, however, write "$200.00." Decimal points are needed only for non-even-dollar amounts, such as "$200.34."
- Do not use the first-person or second-person point of view (for example, *we, I,* or *you*).
- Avoid rhetorical questions. (Don't you agree?)
- Write out dates.
    - **Correct:** January 31, 2003
    - **Incorrect:** 1/31/03
    - **Incorrect:** Jan. 31, 2003

Writing Matter-of-Factly

The following are a few final suggestions to help you in developing an authoritative voice.

- **Dispassionate writing.** It is generally necessary to conceal personal emotions. For instance, even if you are outraged by a situation, you should report about the situation matter-of-factly, without expressing your own anger. Displays of emotion in legal writing can make the writer appear unprofessional and irrational. Authoritative legal writing requires the use of logical arguments, not emotional appeals.
- **Objective writing.** It is important to give an objective overview, explaining all sides of an argument without showing clear preference to one side. Just as it is best to avoid emotional arguments, it is necessary to avoid opinionated statements. A legal writer should openly concede to the opposition everything that must be conceded, while logically rebutting everything that can be rebutted. Your writing will be stronger and more authoritative if you use clear facts, rather than opinions, to create your arguments.

- **Impersonal writing.** In legal writing, it is important to focus on the facts, not on the person who is presenting the facts. Legal writing generally is not an appropriate medium for personal anecdotes. Leave yourself out of the text and simply focus on the issues.
- **Trustworthy writing.** Another way to develop an authoritative voice is to use evidence and examples to establish credibility. It is a good idea to cite other sources to show that the ideas being presented are supported by a larger body of research, experience, and knowledge.

SUMMATION

In your writing, strive for messages that are clear and convincing. Strip away excess words, phrases, sentences, and ideas, and focus on the core of your message. Be sure to communicate this message through the use of compelling logical arguments and a voice that is appropriate for the intended audience. With some effort, you can create a message that is credible, memorable, and influential.

Chapter 11

Mechanics: Grammar

MOST PEOPLE USE EVERYDAY ENGLISH without giving much thought to the mechanics involved in the use of language in speech or writing. Every sentence can be broken down into pieces—the parts of speech. A subject and a verb are the staples of a sentence, and to these other elements (such as a direct object) can be added. There is more than one right way to put the pieces together. Different ways of combining words and phrases lead to different effects and different meanings. The key is to put your sentences together in a way that conveys your intended meaning and is not confusing to your readers.

IN THIS CHAPTER	
• **Parts of Speech**	◦ Conjunctions
◦ Nouns	◦ Interjections
◦ Pronouns	• **Using the Parts of Speech**
◦ Adjectives	◦ Subject-Verb Agreement
◦ Verbs	◦ Misplaced Modifiers
◦ Adverbs	◦ Parallelism in Lists
◦ Prepositions	• **Summation**

PARTS OF SPEECH

The ability to recognize the different parts of speech is the first step in improving a writer's use of grammar and other aspects of language. The eight traditional parts of speech are presented below. Keep in mind that these parts of speech are not mutually exclusive. A noun can sometimes function as an adjective, or a common preposition may function in some sentences as an adverb.

Nouns

A noun represents a person, place, or thing, either abstract (love, dreams) or concrete (Minnesota, table). Nouns are classified as either common or proper. Common nouns refer to generic people, places, or things ("girl," "river," "car"), whereas proper nouns are specific ("Helen," "Mississippi River," "Model T"). Proper nouns are capitalized, whereas common nouns are not. A noun also has a plural form and a possessive form.

Nouns serve as either subjects or objects in sentences. When functioning as the subject, a noun represents the person, place, or thing about which the statement is being made. It is often the source of the action represented by the verb. Although the subject typically comes before the verb, it can fall anywhere in the sentence. A noun can also serve as the object (the person or thing being acted upon) of a sentence or the object of a phrase (such as a prepositional phrase).

- The trial (subject) has begun.
- High in a tree (object of preposition) hung the evidence (subject) she was looking for.

- The car crash (subject) greatly affected Sandy and her boyfriend (objects of sentence).
- Place the files (object of sentence) in the judge's office (object of prepositional phrase).

In the last example above, "you"(which is implied and does not appear) is the subject. *Files* are the things being placed; thus, "files" is the object of the sentence. "In" is a preposition, making "in the judge's office" a prepositional phrase. "Office" is the noun that serves as the object of the phrase.

Pronouns

Pronouns are words that replace nouns to avoid repetition and wordiness. It is important to make clear whom or what the pronoun is referring to. In general, a pronoun follows the noun it represents. One of the most important things to remember is that the form of a personal pronoun changes based on number, case, and point of view. These changes are indicated in the charts below.

Singular Pronouns

	Case		
	Possessive	*Nominative*	*Objective*
First person	mine, my	I	me
Second person	yours, your	you	you
Third person	its, her, hers, his	it, she, he	it, her, him

Plural Pronouns

	Case		
	Possessive	*Nominative*	*Objective*
First person	ours, our	we	us
Second person	yours, your	you	you
Third person	theirs, their	they	them

Adjectives

An adjective is a descriptive word that modifies, quantifies, or otherwise describes a noun or pronoun. Adjectives often, though not always, appear before the word they modify. Predicate adjectives follow the verb but modify the subject (as in "He feels *bad*"). Adjectives are underlined in the examples that follow.

- The *revised* agreement has *innovative* features.
- He was smoking a *Cuban* cigar and eating *french* fries during the *October 31* festivities.
- There are *twenty-four* hours in a day.

Verbs

The verb is the most important part of speech; it represents an action or the presence of some condition. A verb is the only part of speech that can stand alone as a complete sentence (for example, "Go!"). When using verbs, it is important to pay attention to voice, tense, and number.

Voice

Verbs can be used in either active voice or passive voice. Active voice indicates that the subject performs the action ("The jury returned a verdict"), whereas passive voice is used when the subject is the recipient of the action ("A verdict was returned by the jury"). Stylistically, active voice is preferable to passive voice.

Tense

Tense refers to a verb's capacity to express a time frame: present, past, or future. There are also three other, comparatively remote tenses: present perfect, past perfect, and future perfect.

- **Present tense:** They *wait* for the police to arrive.
- **Past tense:** They *waited* for the police to arrive.
- **Future tense** (uses *will*)**:** They *will wait* for the police to arrive.
- **Present perfect tense** (uses *have* or *has*)**:** They *have waited* for the police for thirty minutes.

- **Past perfect tense** (uses *had*)**:** By the time the police arrived, they *had waited* fifty minutes.
- **Future perfect tense** (uses *will have*)**:** When the clock strikes midnight, they *will have waited* an hour and a half to be interviewed by the police.

Number

Verbs can be either singular or plural and should agree in number with the subject of the sentence. See the discussion of subject-verb agreement later in the chapter.

Verb Phrases

Sometimes two verbs (an auxiliary verb and a principal verb) are combined to create a verb phrase ("could prevent" or "may be raining"). When an adverb is used to modify a verb phrase, it should be placed directly after the first auxiliary verb ("could conceivably prevent" or "may already be raining").

To Be

The verb "to be" takes a variety of forms: *is, are, was, were, been, being, be,* and *am.* A form of the infinitive (the verb in its basic, uninflected form) "to be" can be used either as the principal verb (where it would carry the meaning "exist") or as an auxiliary verb (representing continuing action). A form of "to be" is also commonly used as a linking verb to connect the subject with some descriptive word or phrase.

- "That cannot *be*," the defendant is quoted as saying.
- The defendant *is* waiting patiently for a verdict.
- Mr. Taylor *is* guilty.

Adverbs

An adverb is a word that describes, qualifies, or otherwise modifies a verb, an adjective, or another adverb. Often, adverbs end with the suffix *ly*. Not all adverbs end in *ly*, however, and not all words ending in *ly* are adverbs. In the following examples the adverbs are underlined.

- Her lawyer could have argued the case <u>more effectively</u>. ("Effectively" modifies the verb "could have argued," and "more" qualifies the adverb "effectively.")

- That argument was somewhat effective. ("Somewhat" modifies the adjective "effective.")
- According to my secretary, the defendant arrived here at 6:00 p.m. ("Here" modifies the verb "arrived.")
- We got an early start on the investigations and therefore had our argument compiled early. (The first "early" is an adjective modifying the noun "start." The second "early" is an adverb that modifies the verb "had compiled.")

Prepositions

Prepositions link an object (a noun or pronoun) with another word in the sentence and explain how those two words are related. The defining characteristic of a preposition is that it always has an object. The preposition generally comes before the object. Some commonly used prepositions are presented below.

Many prepositions are quite basic.

- *About, above, after, around, as, at, before, between, by, down, except, for, in, of, on, through, to, without*

Sometimes participial forms of words (those ending in *ing*) function as prepositions.

- *Assuming, concerning, considering, during, notwithstanding, regarding, speaking*

Two or more words can work as a unit to form a phrasal preposition.

- *According to, because of, for the sake of, in addition to, in case of, in regard to, in spite of, instead of, with regard to*

A preposition joins with its object and any words that modify the object to form a prepositional phrase. These phrases can function as nouns, adverbs, or adjectives. It is important to pay attention to the placement of prepositional phrases. Those serving as adverbs or adjectives should be placed as closely as possible to the word they are intended to modify. When a prepositional phrase applies equally to all items in a series, the phrase should be placed after the last item of the series. The prepositional phrases are underlined in the sentences below.

- **Correct:** Is the lawyer with glasses and blonde hair here?
- **Incorrect:** Is the lawyer here with glasses and blonde hair?
- **Correct:** The date and time for the trial have been set.
- **Incorrect:** The date for the trial and the time have been set.

Traditionally, it has been viewed as grammatically incorrect to end a sentence with a preposition. However, this rule has no grammatical basis and now is largely ignored.

Conjunctions

Conjunctions are connecting words, serving to join sentences, clauses, or words within a clause. There are two main types of conjunctions.

Coordinating conjunctions join two items of corresponding grammatical rank, such as two independent clauses or two nouns. Conjunctions sometimes appear in the form of a single word or phrase, and other times as paired terms. Some commonly used conjunctions are listed and underlined below.

- *And, also, as a result, but, consequently, for, moreover, nevertheless, no less than, nor, or, otherwise, so, so that, still, therefore, yet*
  - The agreement requested grants and aid for agricultural development.
  - The resident violated her lease; consequently, she must forfeit her security deposit.
- *Both/and, either/or, if/then, neither/nor, not only/but also*
  - A case may be settled either inside or outside of court.

Subordinating conjunctions join two clauses that differ in grammatical rank. Such a conjunction is used to introduce a dependent clause and to indicate the relationship of that clause to the main clause. Subordinating conjunctions may designate a relationship of comparative degree, time, reason, or place.

- *Because, as much as, before, since, without, unless, in order that*
  - He could not say when the case would be closed.
  - Until you file a grievance, there is not much we can do.

As with prepositions, it has traditionally been viewed as incorrect to start a sentence with one of the conjunctions *but, and,* or *so.* Once again, this rule has no grammatical foundation and can be overlooked.

Interjections

Interjections are exclamations (words, phrases, or clauses) that reveal strong feeling. Interjections are generally set apart from the rest of the sentence by some form of punctuation (a comma or exclamation point, for example) and often can stand alone as complete sentences. Interjections are primarily used in dialogue and poetry; thus, they are unlikely to appear frequently in legal writing. The interjections are underlined in the sentences below.

- Well, I warned her this would happen.
- Oh no! I locked my keys in the car.

USING THE PARTS OF SPEECH

The most important consideration in using the parts of speech is to put your words together in ways that clearly communicate your intended meaning. Following are three common types of error that can either impede clarity or compromise the integrity of a written piece. Beware of these not necessarily obvious mistakes. For more tips on avoiding common errors, see Chapter 17.

Subject-Verb Agreement

Writers must pay attention to subject-verb agreement. The number implicit in the subject dictates the number of the verb. Words or phrases that appear between the subject and verb often can be distracting or deceiving, as in the examples below (where subjects and verbs are underlined). As the last two examples illustrate, the number of the verb is not always straightforward and involves some discretion (and a little controversy).

- The *cast* of characters involved in the crime *includes* two former employees.
- The *statute* of limitations *defines* the time frame that is applicable.

- A *variety* of influenza, according to doctors, *was* responsible for the outbreak. (Refers to a specific variety.)
- A *variety* of theories *have been advanced* to explain the phenomenon. (The thing advanced is not the variety but the theories.)

Misplaced Modifiers

A descriptive phrase appearing at the beginning of a sentence may have no clear connection to a noun. Typically, this occurs when the phrase is not immediately followed by the noun it is meant to describe. It is best to place a descriptive word or phrase as close as possible to the word it is intended to modify.

- **Clear:** After staying up all night, Howard was not looking forward to entering the courtroom.
- **Unclear:** After staying up all night, the courtroom seemed unbearable to Howard. (Who or what stayed up all night? The courtroom?)

Parallelism in Lists

Consistency should be applied to items in a list. Essentially, the items in the list should all take the same form—all verbs, all nouns, all complete sentences, or all recommendations. Inconsistency can cause confusion and appear unprofessional.

- **Correct:** Serving on a jury requires dedication, attentiveness, impartiality, and obedience.
- **Incorrect:** Serving on a jury requires dedication, remaining attentive, to be impartial, and obedient.

SUMMATION

There is much variation among the parts of speech. A verb may appear as a word or a phrase, it may be active or passive, and it may vary in tense and number. In addition to this variation within individual elements, the elements can be combined in any number of ways, some more effective than others. To maximize the effectiveness of your writing, study and practice the general principles of grammar, and always strive for clarity.

Chapter 12

Mechanics: Punctuation

PUNCTUATION PROVIDES ORDER TO WRITTEN words. When punctuation rules are not followed, writing becomes confusing and unclear, leading to miscommunication. Writing well not only makes your thoughts easier to understand, but lends you credibility and respect. It is necessary to learn the rules that govern words in order to become an effective writer. With practice, these rules will become automatic and natural.

The punctuation rules included in this chapter are far from exhaustive, but they do address some of the most common issues that arise in writing. Consult a style book, such as *The Chicago Manual of Style,* for more specific punctuation concerns.

IN THIS CHAPTER	
• **Periods** ◦ Periods with Abbreviations ◦ Double Periods • **Question Marks** • **Commas** ◦ Commas with Lists or Series of Items ◦ Commas with Dates and Addresses ◦ Commas with Direct Addresses ◦ Commas with Phrases, Clauses, and Interjections ◦ Commas with Double Adjectives • **Semicolons** ◦ Semicolons with Independent Clauses ◦ Semicolons with Complex Lists	• **Colons** • **Hyphens and Dashes** ◦ Hyphens ◦ Dashes • **Apostrophes** ◦ Forming Contractions ◦ Indicating Possession • **Parentheses and Brackets** ◦ Punctuation in Relation to Parentheses and Brackets • **Quotation Marks** ◦ Punctuation in Relation to Quotation Marks • **Summation**

PERIODS

The period represents finality of thought and is primarily used to mark the end of a declarative or imperative statement. It is also used between the letters of many abbreviations. In a typed manuscript, a period should be followed by a single space.

Periods with Abbreviations

In general, use periods when an abbreviation includes lowercase letters (such as *a.m.*) but not when the abbreviation is in all capital letters (such as *AM*). The abbreviations *Assoc., Bros., Inc.,* and *Co.* should end with periods; *EU* and *WTO* do not need periods. A number of exceptions do exist. For instance, a person's initials should always use periods (such as *A. R. Wesley*). Academic degrees and the abbreviation *U.S.* have traditionally appeared with periods; the periods can be omitted, however, unless they are needed for consistency. Scientific writing omits all periods, but when English units of measure appear in non-scientific writing, periods are generally used (for example, *cu. yd.* to stand for *cubic yard*).

Double Periods

It is never appropriate to use two periods in a row, not even when an abbreviation (such as *p.m.*) marks the end of a sentence. A period and comma may be used together, but it is never appropriate to pair a period with a question mark or exclamation mark.

QUESTION MARKS

Question marks are primarily used to mark direct questions. Sometimes these questions stand alone, and at other times they appear within sentences. When a question appears in the middle of a sentence, it does not need to start with a capital letter.

- Who is that witness?
- The question, who is that witness? was on everyone's mind.

With indirect and courtesy questions, question marks are not needed. Courtesy questions are requests phrased as questions. When the indirect question consists of a single word (such as *who, when, how,* or *why*), the question mark can be omitted, and the word is sometimes italicized.

- Would this day ever end was the question on her mind.
- He needed to know *why*.
- Will you please raise your right hand.

COMMAS

It takes good judgment to use the comma well. The comma represents the smallest break in sentence structure, indicating a slight pause. Although there are many rules regarding comma usage, the end goal is to have a text that is precise, easy to read, and comprehensible. This section discusses comma usage in relation to lists, dates and addresses, direct addresses, phrases and clauses, and double adjectives.

Commas with Lists or Series of Items

In a series of items, a comma should appear between consecutive items in the series, including a comma before the conjunction that joins the final two items. Some writing styles do not require a comma before the final conjunction, but this can impede clarity. A comma is not needed before the first item in a list or after the last item of the list, only between items.

- **Correct:** We met with Andrew Canada, Paul Kellogg, and Lewis McIver.
- **Incorrect:** We met with Andrew Canada, Paul Kellogg and Lewis McIver.
- **Incorrect:** We met with, Andrew Canada, Paul Kellogg, and Lewis McIver.

An exception occurs when the items in a series are all joined by conjunctions. In that case, commas are not needed unless pauses are intended.

- Andrew Canada or Paul Kellogg or Lewis McIver

Another exception occurs when one or more items in the series include internal commas. In that case, semicolons are needed to separate the main items.

Commas with Dates and Addresses

In writing dates using the American format of month-day-year, commas should appear both before and after the year. However, if you are using the day-month-year system, as is customary in some countries, no comma is needed. Additionally, no comma is needed if you are stating only a month and year or if you are referencing a specific day (such as a holiday).

- The contract was signed on March 22, 1997, to implement the company's new policies.
- This information is based on journal entries from 7 November 1988 and 18 February 2000.
- The accident happened on Christmas Eve 2006 in front of the courthouse.

Commas should be used to separate a city from a state or to separate elements of an address when that address appears within text. No comma should be used before a postal code.

- The plane landed in Nairobi, Kenya, at 9 a.m. that day.
- He posted a letter to 303 Chambers Street SW, Waukegan, IL 61589, on the following morning.

Commas with Direct Addresses

When one is addressing a person or a group of people directly, that address (maybe a person's name or a general term, such as "friends") must be set off with commas. This should be done regardless of whether the address comes at the beginning, in the middle, or at the end of a sentence.

- Sir, your response was vague and precludes me from giving an explanation at this time.
- The information presented here, Justice Garman, should help you better understand the cause of death.
- I hope you will consider this new information, Ms. Lowery.
- Dear Amy Lewis,

Commas with Phrases, Clauses, and Interjections

Phrases and clauses are parts of sentences. A clause has both a subject and a verb; a phrase does not. A clause can be either independent or dependent. Independent clauses can stand alone as complete sentences. Dependent ones, on the other hand, require another clause to complete their meaning.

Introductory phrases are usually followed by a comma, except when the phrase is very short or immediately precedes the verb it modifies. A dependent clause located at the beginning of a sentence should always be set off with commas.

- **Introductory phrase:** In October of 1998, Mary Hall was an excited 12-year-old girl.
- **Dependent clause that precedes main clause:** If the plaintiff honors our requests, we will settle outside of court.

Phrases, clauses, and descriptive words are often preceded and/or followed by a comma(s), particularly when a slight pause is intended. It is important, however, to differentiate between essential and nonessential descriptions. Phrases, clauses, and descriptive words are considered essential when their absence would alter the basic meaning of a sentence. If ever in doubt, use a comma to indicate a pause.

- Essential phrases and clauses should not be enclosed in commas. (The word, phrase, or clause in question is underlined below.)
  - Two students cheated and were therefore disqualified.
  - The man with the black briefcase evaded the police.
  - We will agree to the proposal if you accept our conditions.
- Nonessential descriptions, on the other hand, should be enclosed in commas.
  - All of the students were, therefore, disqualified.
  - Her husband, who was carrying a black briefcase, stepped onto the 9:30 bus.
  - The most provocative, if not the most important, part of the statement came last.

When two independent clauses are joined by a conjunction (such as *and, but, or, so, yet*), a comma is generally placed before the conjunction. The comma can be omitted when the two clauses are very short and closely related.

- Ministers salute the historic achievements represented here, and they believe it will strengthen the world economy.

Commas with Double Adjectives

When two or more adjectives precede a noun, those adjectives are generally separated by a comma if they could be joined by *and* without changing the sentence's meaning. A comma should also be used when the same adjective is repeated. (The double adjectives are underlined below.)

- It proved to be a long, exhausting trial.
- The victim rejected traditional religious affiliation.
- Many, many people have experienced this before.

SEMICOLONS

The semicolon falls somewhere in the middle—weaker than a period, yet stronger than a comma. The semicolon has two primary functions: connecting two independent clauses and simplifying complex lists.

Semicolons with Independent Clauses

It is acceptable to join together two complete yet interrelated sentences (two independent clauses). Remember that two independent clauses joined by a conjunction are separated by a comma. When two independent clauses are not joined by a conjunction, however, a semicolon is used. Be careful to avoid using a semicolon with a fragment.

- **Correct:** When Kelli returned home from the store, her mailbox was missing; in its place was a deep hole.
- **Incorrect:** When Kelli returned home from the store, her mailbox was missing; which led her to call the police.

Semicolons with Complex Lists

In a complicated series of items where there is a comma within one or more of the items of the list, it is clearer to place a semicolon between the main items.

- The defendant pleaded that his house had recently, and unexpectedly, caught on fire; that his landlord, whom he had been loyal to for four years, was threatening him with eviction; and that he had just gotten over pneumonia, for which he had been hospitalized.
- She has lived in Syracuse, New York; Bar Harbor, Maine; Pasadena, California; and St. Louis, Missouri.

COLONS

The colon is primarily used to introduce one or more things that illustrate or elaborate upon the information preceding the colon. It can even be used in place of a period to introduce a sequence of related sentences. Colons are most often used to introduce and set off lists.

- At each of the first three stages, products should be chosen from each of the following categories: tops and yarns, fabrics, made-up textile products, and clothing.

Formal salutations (in a letter or speech, for example) should also be followed by a colon.

- To Whom It May Concern:
- Dear Justice Carmon:

HYPHENS AND DASHES

Hyphens and dashes are used to connect compound words and to set off explanations or lists. It is important to differentiate between the hyphen and the dash (represented by double hyphens if necessary because of limited capabilities).

HYPHENS

Hyphens (-) are used to form compound words and to separate numbers or letters. A compound word is formed when two or more descriptive words work together as a unit, often to modify a verb or noun. The words that make up these descriptive units are typically combined using hyphens. When uncertain about whether or not to hyphenate descriptive words, try looking them up in the dictionary.

- Twenty-four hours a day
- Non-English-speaking people

Hyphenated words can be used to improve readability and clarity in writing. At times, the same phrase can mean something different with a hyphen than it does without one.

- Much needed clothing (there is a lot of clothing, and it is needed) versus much-needed clothing (the clothing is badly needed, and there may not be a lot of it)

Hyphens are also used to separate numbers (in telephone or social security numbers, for example) or letters (when spelling out a word).

- His last name is Alston; that's a-l-s-t-o-n.

Dashes

Dashes (–) or double hyphens (- -) are used to set off explanatory statements or lists of items (performing a function similar to that of commas, parentheses, or colons).

- The jury—they had been debating this case for months—finally reached a verdict.
- They outlined an agreement—an agreement they hoped would be approved by everyone involved.

APOSTROPHES

Apostrophes have two primary uses: to form contractions and to indicate possession.

Forming Contractions

When two words are combined into one, an apostrophe is used to represent the missing letters.

- *Haven't* instead of *have not*

Indicating Possession

To indicate possession, add an apostrophe followed by an *s* to the end of a singular word, including one that ends in *s*. For plural words already ending with an *s*, simply add an apostrophe (no additional *s* is needed).

- The dog's bone (singular noun, only one dog)
- The dogs' bones (plural noun, more than one dog)
- The octopus's leg (singular noun that happens to end in *s*)

PARENTHESES AND BRACKETS

The function of parentheses is similar to that of commas or dashes: they are used to separate or set off pieces of information. The main difference is that the information enclosed in parentheses is typically less closely related to the rest of the sentence.

Square brackets are typically used within quotations to insert information that was not originally a part of the quoted text. They are helpful for inserting explanations or translations. Brackets are also useful as an alternative to parentheses within parentheses.

It is important to pay attention to the placement of other punctuation (such as commas and periods) in relation to parentheses and brackets.

Punctuation in Relation to Parentheses and Brackets

- **Periods.** When a complete independent sentence is enclosed in parentheses or brackets, the period should be placed within the parentheses or brackets as well. If, however, only part of a sentence lies within the parentheses or brackets, the period should be placed after the closing parenthesis or bracket.
    - (RESIDENT agrees not to smoke inside of the house and is also responsible for prohibiting any guests from smoking within the house.)
    - RESIDENT agrees not to smoke inside of the house (and is also responsible for prohibiting any guests from smoking within the house).
- **Question marks and exclamation points.** These forms of punctuation can be placed either before or after the closing parenthesis or bracket, depending upon the context. When they are part of the parenthetical material, question marks and exclamation points go inside the parentheses. If not explicitly a part of the parenthetical material, these marks should be outside the parentheses.
    - I just realized (why didn't this occur to me before?) that I cannot make it to that court date.
    - When does the ambassador plan to present a first draft of the trade agreement (regarding intellectual property)?

- **Commas, semicolons, and colons.** Commas, semicolons, and colons (when needed) should always be placed after the closing parenthesis or bracket.
    - The defendant missed her court date (without providing a reasonable excuse); therefore, there is a warrant out for her arrest.

QUOTATION MARKS

It is important to differentiate between double quotation marks (“) and single quotation marks (‘). Double quotation marks are used to mark dialogue and direct quotations. Single quotation marks, on the other hand, are used to designate a quotation within a quotation.

In addition to the uses mentioned above, double quotation marks are sometimes used, instead of italics, to indicate titles. Segments of larger works are those that require quotation marks. For example, the following types of titles should be placed within double quotation marks:

- Book chapters
- Poems
- Songs
- Magazine articles
- Newspaper articles

Be sure to pay attention to the placement of other punctuation (such as commas and periods) in relation to quotation marks.

Punctuation in Relation to Quotation Marks

- **Periods.** When a quote or a title in quotation marks ends a sentence, the period should always be placed inside the quotation marks. Do not confuse a single quotation mark with an apostrophe at the end of a word, however.
    - **Correct:** My client believes this is a “disgrace to all humankind.”
    - **Incorrect:** I think this mess is the girls.’
- **Question marks and exclamation points.** With quotations, question marks and exclamation points are used the same way as they are with parentheses: they can be placed

either inside or outside of the quotation marks, depending on the context.

  - The lawyer asked, "Were you alone at the time of the burglary?"
  - Why would the judge say that she is "unfit to stand trial"?

- **Commas.** For a brief quotation, the quoted material is usually introduced by a comma. Longer or more formal quotations, however, are generally introduced by a colon. When a quotation is introduced by *that, whether,* or a similar expression, neither a comma nor a colon is needed. If a comma is called for at the end of a quotation, the comma (like the period) should always be placed before the quotation marks.
  - "I hope you can provide proof of insurance," the officer said to her.
  - Jenny asked her lawyer, "What are my options in this situation?"
  - We are pleased to hear the comment that "the new trade agreement promotes fair trade and special treatment for developing countries."
- **Semicolons and colons.** When needed, semicolons and colons should always follow the quotation marks.
  - The following points are made about colons in Chapter 2, "Punctuation and Grammar Matter": colons are useful for marking introductions and formal salutations, but should not be overused.

SUMMATION

No matter how simple or elegant your writing is, poor use of punctuation can make it confusing and frustrating. Good punctuation, however, enhances your writing—organizing your arguments, enforcing your points, and adding emphasis to your conclusions. Although learning how to use proper punctuation won't by itself make you an effective writer, using it improperly will definitely make your writing less effective. If you've never opened a style manual before, pick one up and consult it before you start writing. The proper use of punctuation will add power to your words, and to your overall message.

Chapter 13

Bullets, Charts, and Demonstrative Aids

AS THEY SAY, "SEEING IS BELIEVING." This common assertion alludes to the power of visual stimuli. Simply hearing about something is often not as convincing or as "real" as seeing it yourself. Images are powerful.

Visual stimuli can carry great weight in the courtroom. Lawyers should consider using visual aids to convince the judge and jury of their arguments. In addition to photographs, charts, and bulleted lists, there are other useful tools for providing visual representation of data or emphasizing main points. When presented effectively, the use of visual aids in advocacy can be invaluable.

IN THIS CHAPTER	
• **Benefits of Visual Aids in Advocacy** ◦ Multiple Communication Channels ◦ Power of Visual Stimuli ◦ Organizing Ideas ◦ Increasing Accessibility	• **Types of Visual Aids** ◦ Charts and Graphs ◦ Bullet Points and Numbers ◦ Images and Objects ◦ Technology-Oriented Media • **Summation**

BENEFITS OF VISUAL AIDS IN ADVOCACY

Bullets, charts, demonstrative aids, and other visual modes of communication are becoming increasingly prevalent in written and oral advocacy. The use of visual aids provides a number of benefits to legal professionals, some of which are discussed below.

Multiple Communication Channels

In addition to oral argument, visual devices provide a second way of making a point or presenting information. In marketing campaigns, advertisers attempt to bombard consumers with information from numerous angles, hoping that at least one of their tactics will be successful. Advertisers may run a print advertisement in the newspaper, air a radio advertisement, produce a 30-second televised commercial, and purchase an online banner advertisement. By using multiple communication channels—print media, radio, television, and the Internet—these advertisers increase their chances of success. Just as advertisers attempt to persuade the public to purchase some product or service, lawyers attempt to convince the court to adopt a particular stance. Thus, bombarding the court from numerous angles may increase a lawyer's chances of success.

By presenting information in more than one way, lawyers can also clarify any confusing or complex points. Imprecise word choices can lead jurors to conjure up their own images of the facts based upon their personalized interpretations. When a lawyer uses pictures or icons to illustrate a point, however, everyone literally sees the same picture and retains the same image. Even if a jury member does not fully grasp a lawyer's words, a chart or photograph can help that person visualize and better understand the situation at hand. Further, retention is often increased when people receive a message via multiple channels. If a person both sees and hears a message, he or she is more likely to retain that message. Thus, there is a better chance that a jury or judge will remember information that is presented in more than one way.

Power of Visual Stimuli

Visual aids engage the eyes as well as the ears. Such a multifaceted, multichannel approach may not be traditional, but it can have a very powerful effect. Some people are visual learners and are more reachable by visual stimuli than by oral arguments. Classroom teaching methods often reflect this understanding; good teachers generally present material in more than one way to reach students with different learning styles. As in the classroom, visual aids are useful for effectively communicating with visual learners in the courtroom.

In certain instances, visual models are simply more forceful than words alone. Consider, for example, explaining a car accident to the court. You could say, "The car sustained a collision on the left side, causing that side to be crushed," or you could show a picture of the actual crash, displaying jagged metal, glass shards, and other debris. In this instance, the picture is likely to be more powerful than the words alone. In another situation, you may say to the court, "The vast majority of witnesses confirmed these events." These words could be made more powerful if they were accompanied by a pie chart that was 90 percent filled in. The use of visual aids can add validity to your case and make it more convincing.

Organizing Ideas

Visual aids, especially bulleted or numbered lists, can help lawyers effectively organize ideas and events. Chapter 9, on organization, briefly discussed the role of bulleted or numbered lists in text. These lists can also be useful as visual aids displayed using PowerPoint or some other means. A bulleted or numbered list can help your audience focus on and remember your main points. Lists can also provide organization by previewing and summarizing the main points of an argument.

Charts, tables, and graphs are other ways to display information in an organized manner. These visuals can show relationships between items and can help the audience mentally categorize information. In the following example, a lawyer is explaining the transactions and relationships that form the backdrop of a plaintiff's claims. The demonstrative instrument provides visual explanations to clarify complex transactions.

WRITTEN EXPLANATION

In July 2001 Heartland Company, owned by Daniel Jones, and a PREA affiliate, received a loan for $2 million. The loan was issued as a secured note by PREFSA, lender to PREA. Later in July 2001 Heartland exchanged the $2 million for assets from Necessities Inc. Necessities is owned by John Smith and operated by Mr. and Mrs. Smith. Necessities was a PREA affiliate until 2006. In late February 2002 Necessities received a loan for $1.35 million. This loan was also issued as a secured note by PREFSA, lender to PREA. In March 2002 Necessities then exchanged the $1.35 million in addition to $250,000 in the form of a subordinated note for assets from Piper Inc. Piper is owned by Mr. and Mrs. Piper and was a GMAC affiliate until 2004.

Increasing Accessibility

The use of well-designed visual aids can help a presentation seem more professional, accessible, and clear. As mentioned before, visuals can enhance the clarity of a message by illustrating important points. With clearly illustrated points, legal arguments become more accessible and understandable to the general public. These are all desirable goals in the courtroom as the legal field moves toward the plainspoken and accessible.

TYPES OF VISUAL AIDS

There are various types of visual aids that can enhance the effectiveness of a lawyer's arguments in written and oral advocacy.

Charts and Graphs

A chart or graph provides a visual representation of specific, quantifiable data. These visual representations serve to illustrate relationships between different parts of the data and to explain complex information quickly and clearly. There are many different kinds of charts and graphs;

Visual Aid

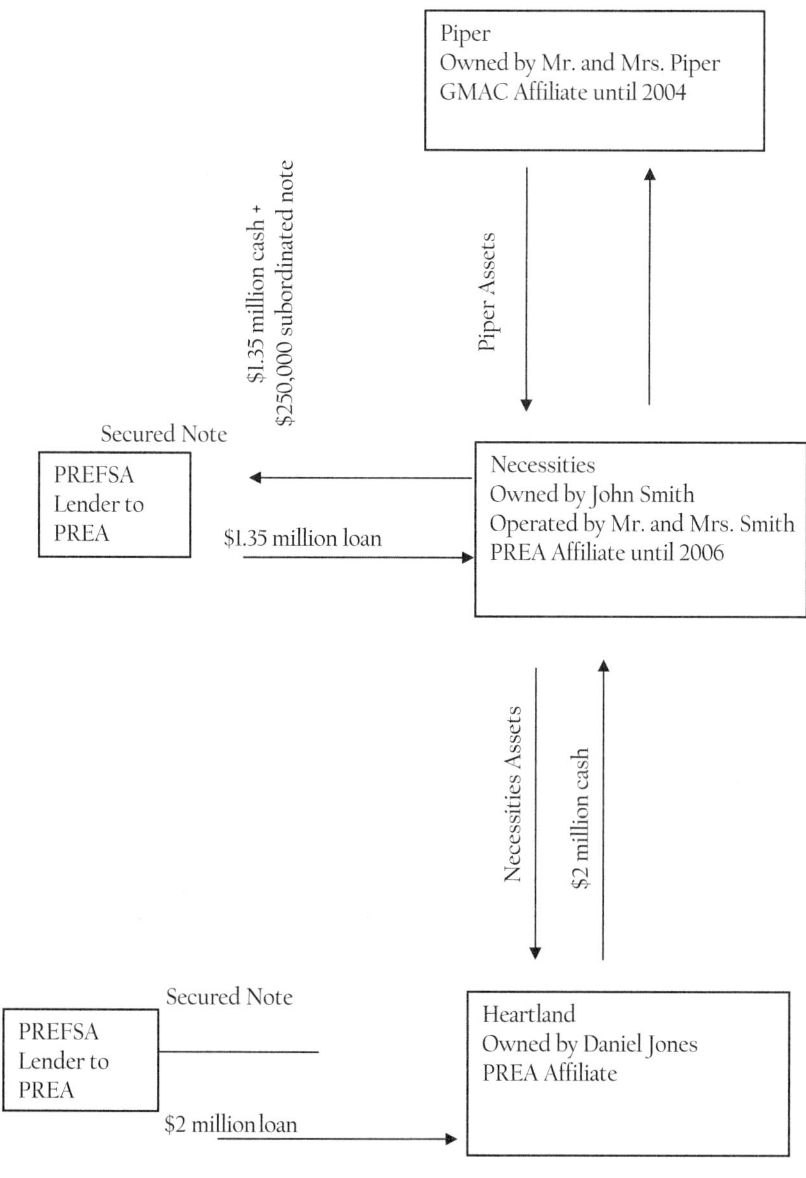

the type of information to be presented should determine the type of chart or graph used, as some charts or graphs are better suited to a particular data set than others. It should be noted that only six of the most common types of charts are discussed below. Many other, less commonly used charts exist as well.

- **Bar graphs.** A bar graph displays frequencies or values for various categories. This type of graph has two or more rectangular bars (that can run either horizontally or vertically), and the length of each bar is proportional to the value it represents. Bar graphs are useful for comparing two or more items.
- **Histograms.** A histogram is a special kind of bar graph that displays frequency distributions and shows what proportion of cases fall into each of several categories. Histograms differ from bar graphs in that it is the *area* of the bar, not the length, that denotes its value. The width of each bar represents the number of classes into which the variable has been divided, and the height of each bar represents frequencies within each class. Histograms are useful for comparing frequencies in large data sets.
- **Scatterplots.** A scatterplot displays relationships between two or more variables. A scatterplot essentially looks like a collection of points. The associated variables determine the location of each point. The value of one variable determines a point's position on the horizontal axis, and the value of another variable determines that point's position on the vertical axis.
- **Line charts.** A line chart is a type of scatterplot that plots a set of ordered observations and then connects the plots with the best-fitting line. A line chart can be used to display patterns. The following example could be used to portray a company's earnings in different years for purposes of establishing the damages caused by a rival's anti-competitive actions. As you will see, the graph is useful for clarifying the written explanation.

WRITTEN EXPLANATION

Yearly earnings for Amnesiac Inc., a manufacturer of automobile parts, had been rising steadily since the company's inception in 1998. During the company's first year in operation, 1998–99, sales were $18 million. Sales nearly doubled in 1999–2000, coming in at $33 million. Sales then rose steadily in the following three years, climbing to $48 million

Visual Aid

Earnings for Amnesiac Incorporated 1998–2007

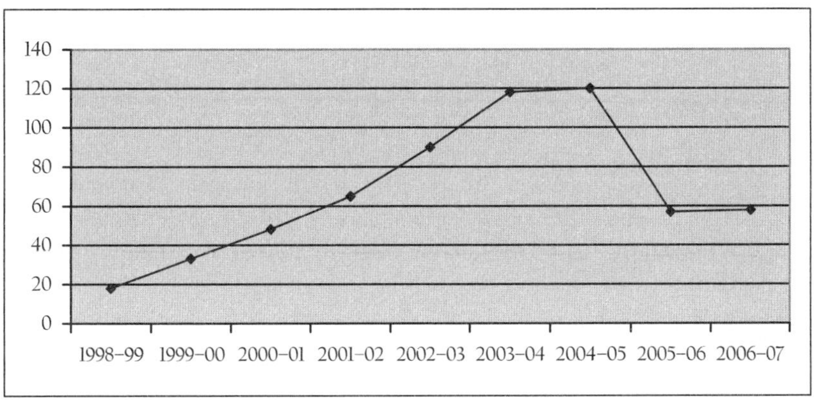

in 2000–01, $65 million in 2001–02, and $90 million in 2002–03. The 2003–04 and 2004–05 fiscal years saw the company reap record profits, reaching $118 million in 2003–04 and $120 million in 2004–05.

In 2005 Amnesiac's competitor Rawlings Inc. signed exclusive contracts with three major automobile manufacturers, taking away significant business from Amnesiac. These anti-competitive actions caused Amnesiac's yearly earnings to drop 52.5 percent between 2004–05 and 2005–06. The company's yearly earnings dropped to $57 million in 2005–06, and they remained at $58 million in 2006–07.

- **Pie charts.** A pie chart is a circular chart that is divided into pieces or slices, each of which represent a percentage value. Each "piece of the pie" represents a fraction of the whole. The following example could be used to show racial percentages of interviewees and hires for a company with allegedly racially discriminatory hiring practices.

WRITTEN EXPLANATION

In early October 2005, Sadie June and Associates conducted interviews for their annual fall hires. The majority of their interviewees were Caucasian, as is to be expected in the state of Indiana, where Caucasians make up over 88 percent of the state population. There was a good deal of diversity in the interview process, though, with 46 percent of interviewees being Caucasian, 23.6 percent Asian, 23 percent African American, and 7 percent other ethnicities.

This same level of diversity was not represented in the company's hiring practices, however. Of new hires, 72 percent were Caucasian, 21.6 percent Asian, 4.8 percent other ethnicities, and 1.6 percent African American. It seems clear that Caucasian and Asian candidates were largely preferred over African American candidates. African Americans, who make up 6.5 percent of Indiana's state population, were highly represented in the interview pool, making up 23 percent of interviewees. Despite these statistics, only 1.6 percent of new hires were

Visual Aid

Racial Percentages of Interviewees

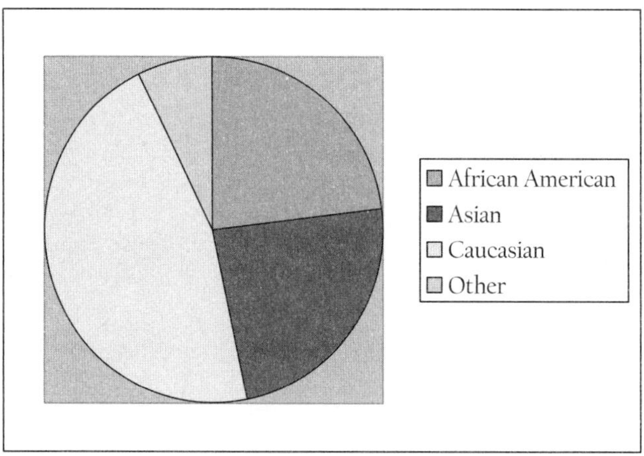

Racial Percentages of New Hires

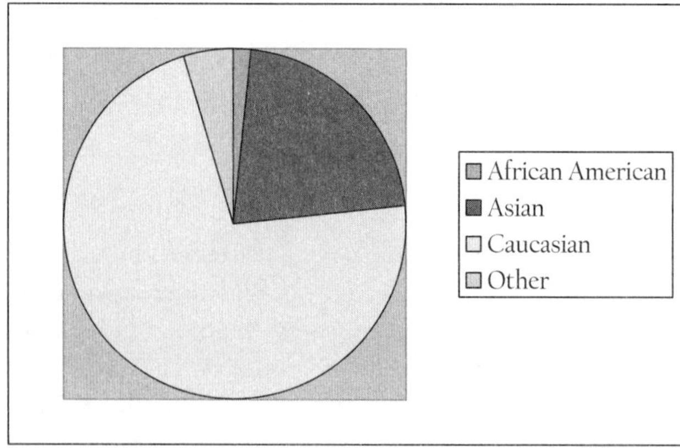

African Americans. Caucasians, on the other hand, made up 46 percent of interviewees but 72 percent of new hires.

- **Timeline.** A timeline is a linear, graphical representation of a chronological sequence of events. This type of chart uses points to represent the most important events of a particular time frame.

Bullet Points and Numbers

As mentioned previously, bullet points and numbers can make your arguments appear more organized and can help listeners focus on your main ideas. Be sure to use these tools wisely, however. Remember that simple bullets, such as basic dots or boxes, are preferred over symbols such as arrows or checkmarks. Simple bullets are more professional and less distracting. Also be sure to keep bulleted lists short. This is particularly important when you are using a bulleted or numbered list during an oral presentation. Your bulleted points should consist only of a short phrase that represents your main point. You should then expand upon that phrase in your oral explanation. If your bullet point includes complete sentences, it will become cluttered and unfocused.

Correct

REASONS TO IMPEACH PRESIDENT GEORGE W. BUSH
• Used deception to lead the country into an unjust war • Allowed friends and business partners to profit off of war • Authorized torture and rendition of prisoners of war and suspected terrorist • Denied American citizens their constitutional rights • Failed to defend our homeland and its borders

Incorrect

REASONS TO IMPEACH PRESIDENT GEORGE W. BUSH
• George W. Bush lied about his motives and led Congress as well as the American people into an unjust war in Iraq. • Throughout the war in Iraq, President Bush has been unethical in allowing his friends and business partners to profit off the war.

- The president authorized torture and rendition of prisoners of war and suspected terrorists in Iraq, which constitutes a complete violation of the Geneva Conventions, a treaty signed by the United States and therefore part of American law.
- President Bush has violated the constitutional rights of American citizens by holding people without charge, performing illegal wiretapping, denying citizens a fair trial, and not allowing people to face their accusers.
- President George W. Bush has failed as president of the United States to defend his country and its borders.

The first example is an effective use of bulleted points because it leaves out specific details and includes only phrases that represent the main points of the argument. A lawyer can then expand upon each idea orally. The second example becomes too busy with the use of complete sentences and the inclusion of too many details. A bulleted or numbered list should not speak for you; it should complement what you have to say.

Images and Objects

As discussed previously, visual stimuli can be more powerful than words alone. Evidence in advocacy can take the form of testimony or tangible evidence. Images and objects constitute tangible evidence. Using images and objects in written and oral advocacy can make your argument more convincing and can help you win the case. For instance, a photo can prove that a certain person was in a particular place at a particular time.

Technology-Oriented Media

When used tastefully, computer programs such as Microsoft PowerPoint can be beneficial in the courtroom. The use of PowerPoint can enhance a case, making it more persuasive and memorable with the use of animation, sound effects, and video testimony. Of course, if used incorrectly, these same effects can be distracting in a court of law. Following are some general guidelines for using PowerPoint effectively.

- Communicate only one message per graphic display. If a single graphic display atempts to communicate multiple messages, it can become confusing and unclear.
- As with bulleted or numbered lists, the use of fewer words is better.

- Every element of a PowerPoint presentation should have a purpose. Avoid things that distract from the purpose, such as unneeded text, arrows, lines, colors, or movement.
- Use color only if it conveys some sort of meaning; avoid using color for aesthetic value.
- Maintain a consistent style and format from one slide to the next. Don't allow inconsistent text or slide formatting to become a distraction.
- When possible, avoid altering photographs. If a photo is altered (such as being cropped or resized), be prepared to give an explanation to the court and your opponent.
- If a document is displayed on the screen, it is useful to underline important text or to add an arrow or circle to draw attention to a particular portion of the document.

SUMMATION

Whether in the form of charts, graphs, physical objects, photographs, or bulleted lists, visual aids can enhance the effectiveness of a written or oral argument. Using visuals successfully can help lawyers convince judges and juries of their arguments.

Chapter 14

Legal Citation Systems

IN ANY ACCOUNT OF SOME event, the source of the information is of critical importance. If it is secondhand information that has been passed along through several people before getting to you, you will be less likely to trust a story than you would if you were given the information by someone witnessing the event firsthand.

In legal writing also, the source of your information is vital. Some readers will disagree with your arguments and want to know where you got your information. If you can demonstrate that the information came from or is supported by trustworthy sources, your claims will be more convincing. If you cannot cite trustworthy sources, however, your arguments will be difficult for readers to accept. It is important to back up all claims and allegations with reliable sources of information.

IN THIS CHAPTER	

• **Styles of Citation**
• **Citing Cases**
  ◦ The Full Citation
  ◦ Unpublished Cases
  ◦ Short Cites
• **Citing Other Common Authorities**
  ◦ Constitutions
  ◦ Statutes
	◦ Law Review Articles
	◦ Restatements
	• **Citation Sentences and Clauses**
	  ◦ Signal Words
	• **Summation**

STYLES OF CITATION

As discussed in Chapter 8 and elsewhere in this book, it is a good idea to cite references to trusted authorities in your writing. Including ideas and quotations from outside sources adds credibility to an argument. The first step is to do some research and locate the authorities you wish to use to support your writing. Once your research is complete and sources have been located, you must determine how to properly cite those authorities in briefs and other court documents. Using the citation information you have provided, readers should have enough details to locate the cited sources and consult the authorities themselves.

Of the many different styles of citation, the two most commonly used in the legal field are *Bluebook* (by the Harvard Law Review) and *ALWD* (Association of Legal Writing Directors Manual). Individual courts often specify which citation style they prefer. Thus, you will need to become familiar with the guidelines of the specific court(s) you are working with.

Of course, there are various differences from one style of citation to the next and from one court to the next. Legal citation is an extensive topic that cannot be covered in a single chapter; thus this chapter is intended to serve only as a general introduction to the principles of legal citation. Locate a copy of *Bluebook* or *ALWD* for specific citation rules.

CITING CASES

Court cases are perhaps the most important sources cited in legal writing. Past court cases establish the common law and interpret statutes and codes. These interpretations determine what particular statutes mean in various factual scenarios. Court cases are the fundamental building blocks of all legal argument and analysis. Essentially, case citations make up "the Holy Bible for practicing attorneys." As we begin discussing the specifics of citation, note that all examples used in this chapter are for purposes of illustration only; they are not from actual cases.

The Full Citation

The first time a case is cited, it should always be cited in full. The full citation of a case consists of three parts: the case title (always appearing in italics or underlined in some style systems), information telling the reader where to find the case, and a parenthetical note giving the name of the court and the date.

- **The case title.** A case is titled using the last names of the involved parties (for example, *Johnson v. Richardson*) or the names of the corporate or governmental entities in the litigation (or a mixture of the two). If there are multiple parties involved, use only the first named party on each side. In standard text sentences, titles are always italicized or underlined. In some styles, case titles in pure citations (appearing as text interjections or in footnotes) are not italicized. This book will use the convention of italicizing full case titles.
    - **Correct:** *Matthews v. Kensington*
    - **Correct:** *Matthews v. Katherine Kensington and Co.*
    - **Incorrect:** *Janice Matthews v. Katherine Kensington*
    - **Incorrect:** *Matthews, Pitaya, and Gonzalez v. Kensington*
- **The case's location.** Following the case title, information about the reporter is given. Reporters are sources that publish cases. This information should be given in the following order: volume, name of reporter, page number. No commas should be used, and none of this information should be italicized or underlined. The citation below indicates that the case begins on page 399 of Volume 12 of the *Federal Reporter*, third series.
    - 12 F. 3d 399

- Sometimes a case is documented in more than one reporter. In this situation, a citation should be given for each reporter, and the citations should be separated by commas. Also consider the order of the citations. The highest and most recent authority should appear first, followed in descending order by authorities that are less recent and hold less power.
    - 347 U.S. 483, 74 S. Ct. 686, 98 L. Ed. 873
- Sometimes a writer may wish to cite only a particular point in the opinion, rather than the opinion as a whole. When this is the case, both the page number of the specific point being referenced and the page number that marks the start of the opinion should be cited. The citation should appear in the same format as above, except the page number for the specific point being cited should appear at the end of the citation and should be separated from the opening page by a comma. The citation below indicates that the case begins on page 399, but that the specific quotation being used is found on page 403.
    - 12 F. 3d 399, 403
- **Court and date.** The third part of a case citation names the court that decided the case and the year the case was published. An abbreviation for the court as well as the year of publication should be provided in parentheses.
    - **Federal district court.** Each federal district court has its own abbreviation. You can locate a list of these abbreviations or determine the abbreviation using the following guidelines.

      The abbreviation for *district* is "D." District courts are determined by geography, so an abbreviation is needed to represent the geographical region of the court: Central (C.), Eastern (E.), Middle (M.), Northern (N.), Southern (S.), or Western (W.). To form the full abbreviation for a U.S. district court, place the geographic designation before the *D*, and then add the state abbreviation after the *D*. (Take care to use the appropriate state abbreviation. Note that the approved state abbreviations are not always the standard U.S. Postal Service abbreviations.)

The first example below indicates that the Federal District Court for the Southern District of New York published the opinion in 1987. The second example indicates that the Federal District Court of Hawaii published the opinion in 1993.

- (S.D.N.Y. 1987)
- (D. Haw. 1993)

o **Federal circuit court.** Abbreviations for federal circuit courts are formed by using the abbreviation "Cir." preceded by one of the following: 1st, 2d, 3d, 4th, 5th, 6th, 7th, 8th, 9th, 10th, 11th, D.C., or Fed. The example below indicates that the Federal Court of Appeals for the Fifth Circuit published the opinion in 1999.

- (5th Cir. 1999)

o **U.S. Supreme Court.** The abbreviation for the U.S. Supreme Court is "U.S." Because Supreme Court cases are recorded in their own special recorder (U.S. and S. Ct.), there is no need to include the court abbreviation in parentheses. Readers will be able to determine which court decided the case based on the reporter, and including the court abbreviation in parentheses would be redundant. Thus, the parenthetical should include only the date.

- **Correct:** 347 U.S. 48, 74 S. Ct. 68, 98 L. Ed. 873 (1954)
- **Incorrect:** 347 U.S. 48, 74 S. Ct. 68, 98 L. Ed. 873 (U.S. 1954)

o **Highest court of state.** For cases decided in the highest court of state, the state abbreviation and the year should be included in parentheses. If, however, the court is obvious from one of the reporters, then do not put the court's abbreviation in parentheses. For instance, if the reporter includes only cases from one particular court, then the court will be obvious, and only the date is needed in parentheses.

        - (Ill. 1987)
        - (Alaska 2005)
        - 523 N.Y.S.2d 140 (1965)
    - **Lower state courts.** Abbreviation styles for lower state courts vary by state and court, so it is always best to look them up. The following example indicates a decision published by the Louisiana Fourth Circuit Court of Appeals in 1988.
        - (La. App. 4 Cir. 1988)

Thus, a full citation of a court case includes three things—case title, case location, and parenthetical with court and date. Putting the pieces together, a full citation may look like one of the following.

- *Matthews v. Kensington,* 12 F. 3d 399 (D. Haw. 1993)
- *Candy Young and Co. v. Pritchard,* 347 U.S. 48, 74 S. Ct. 68, 98 L. Ed. 873 (1954)

Unpublished Cases

In your research, you may come across court decisions that are not published in a reporter. The unpublished case may be a recent opinion, for example, and there is a time lag between the completion of a written opinion and its appearance in a printed reporter. Other cases, particularly those from some intermediate appellate state courts, are never formally published but can still be accessed via electronic databases such as Lexis and Westlaw. Jurisdictions are increasingly treating these unpublished cases as equivalent to published ones. In many courts, it is acceptable to cite an unpublished case. Of course, the citations for these cases will look different from those above because there is no reporter information to include. A citation for an unpublished case should include the following elements:

- **The case title.** This will be the same as described and illustrated above.
- **The court's docket number for the particular case.** The word "docket" refers to the schedule of court proceedings. It is informally used to refer to the court calendar

or the caseload as a whole. "Docket" can also mean the register that contains court proceedings. In essence, the docket provides a tracking system for various court cases. Each case is given a docket number (also known as the case number), which may look like one of the examples below.

- No. 03-21412
- CRB-01-077298

- **The document's database number.** A document's database number consists of three parts: the year, a database identifier, and the document number. All of this information can be found at the beginning of a Lexis or Westlaw document. Examples of database identifiers are the following.
  - "WL" is the database identifier for Westlaw.
  - Database identifiers for Lexis vary depending on which specific Lexis database is being used. For example, "U.S. Dist. Lexis" is the identifier for the Lexis database covering U.S. district court cases.
- When all database information is combined (year, database identifier, and document number), the citation may look like the example below. No commas are used between these three pieces of information, and none of this information is italicized.
  - 2008 WL 5039650
- **Court and full date of opinion.** In parentheses, the following information should be given: abbreviation for the court where the decision was made and full date of decision. The date should appear in the month-day-year format.
  - (5th Cir. Nov. 5, 2007)

A full citation for an unpublished case may look like one of the examples below. Commas should separate the case title from the court docket number and the court docket number from the database information.

- *Smith v. Jones*, No. 03-21412, 2008 WL 5039650 (5th Cir. Nov. 5, 2007)

- *James v. Colorado,* CRB-01-077298, 2005 U.S. Dist. Lexis 2597016 (Colo. App. July 28, 2004)

Short Cites

After a case has been cited in full once, it is appropriate thereafter to use a short form of the citation. It is necessary to cite the case in full only the first time the case is mentioned. In nearly all legal styles shortened case references are always italicized.

- When referring to a case generally, simply use the last name of the first named party. For a case titled *Johnson v. Richardson,* you would need to use only *Johnson.*
- When citing information from a specific page of a court case, it is necessary to include slightly more information. The following form would be used to indicate that the specific information or quotation being referred to came from page 403.
    - *Johnson,* 12 F. 3d at 403
- When the most recent citation was from the same case, use *Id.* in place of the case name. (The abbreviation *Id.* is short for *Ibidem,* the Latin term meaning "in the same place," and should be italicized.)
    - *Id.* at 403

CITING OTHER COMMON AUTHORITIES

In addition to court cases, legal writing often cites information from constitutions, statutes, law review articles, and restatements.

Constitutions

Citations for state constitutions begin with the name of the state, while a citation for the U.S. Constitution begins with the abbreviation "U.S." The article and section where the information was found should follow the state or country name. No italics are used for citing constitutions.

- Miss. Const. art. 3, sect. 1

Statutes

Different types of statutes are cited differently. For citing the U.S. Code (federal statutes), the form below should be used. Note that the second example is a citation to the annotated U.S. Code. The symbol in each citation stands for "section."

- 12 U.S.C. § 429 (1999)
- 12 U.S.C. Ann. § 429 (1999)

Each state has a particular statute notation. One example for Louisiana is given below.

- 3 La. Rev. Stat. 129 (1996)

Following is how a citation should appear when referring to rules of procedure and evidence. The example below refers specifically to Federal Rule of Civil Procedure 11.

- Fed. R. Civ. P. 11

Law Review Articles

Citations for law review articles first cite the author's name and the article title. Each piece of information is followed by a comma, and the article title should be italicized. Next should be the volume number, journal title (typically abbreviated according to some scheme), page number, and date. These four pieces of information should not be separated by commas, and the date should appear in parentheses. Note that only the article title, not the journal title, is italicized.

- William Smith, *Joint Liability*, 32 Yale L.J. 299 (1956)

Restatements

A sample citation for a restatement is presented below. Recall that the symbol used stands for "section." *AWLD* uses italics as in the example below, while *Bluebook* does not.

- *Restatement (Second) of Torts* § 333 (1981)

CITATION SENTENCES AND CLAUSES

Once a citation has been constructed, it must be properly incorporated into the text. This can be done with the use of citation sentences and citation clauses. Typically, a legal proposition will be referred to, and then the authority for that proposition will be cited in a separate sentence. A citation sentence is used when the citation applies to the entire sentence preceding. A citation clause, on the other hand, is used when a citation applies only to part of a sentence. Commas should appear directly before and directly after the citation clause. If multiple authorities are cited, consecutive citations should be separated by a semicolon.

- **Citation sentence:** Appellate courts apply a *de novo* standard of review to the legal conclusions of lower courts. *Johnson v. Richardson,* 123 U.S. 90 (1977); *Monty v. Python,* 429 F. 3d 769 (5th Cir. 1982).
- **Citation clause:** Appellate courts apply a *de novo* standard of review to the legal conclusions of lower courts, *Johnson v. Richardson,* 123 U.S. 90 (1977); *Monty v. Python,* 429 F. 3d 769 (5th Cir. 1982), but reverse factual findings only when they are clearly in error.

Signal Words

Citation sentences and clauses are often introduced with signal words. When the cited authority uses the exact same phrasing as used in your writing, no signal words should be used. But whenever the phrasing is not an exact match, a signal word is needed. Below are six of the most common signal words used in legal writing. These signal words should always be italicized. They should be capitalized when they begin a citation sentence. When they appear within a sentence (to introduce a citation clause or to set apart contradictory cases in a citation sentence), no capitalization is used.

- **See.** Start a citation sentence with the word *"See"* if the cited authority contains the same idea but does not use the exact same wording. Use *"see"* before a citation clause:

  - Coverage of third parties under home owners liability requires negligence on the part of the home owner, *see Matthews v. Kensington,* 12 F. 3d 399 (D. Haw. 1993), but this can be overridden if no party is at fault.
- **See also.** A citation sentence should be preceded with *"See also"* when the source contains related information that supports your claim, and similarly for a citation clause:
  - *Johnson v. Richardson,* 123 U.S. 90 (1977); *see also Monty v. Python,* 429 F. 3d 769 (5th Cir. 1982).
- **E.g.** This Latin abbreviation should be used when you are citing several examples to illustrate a general legal rule. Remember that *"e.g."* means "for example" and is always followed by a comma. When appropriate, *e.g.* can be combined with other signal words, as in "*see, e.g.,*" or *"but see, e.g."*

  The first example below lists several cases that illustrate a legal rule, and the writer has used the same wording as in the original text. The second example below also lists several cases illustrating a legal rule, but the cases support the writer's ideas without using the exact same wording.
  - *E.g., Johnson v. Richardson,* 123 U.S. 90 (1977); *Monty v. Python,* 429 F. 3d 769 (5th Cir. 1982); *Matthews v. Kensington,* 12 F. 3d 399 (D. Haw. 1993).
  - *See, e.g., Johnson v. Richardson,* 123 U.S. 90 (1977); *Monty v. Python,* 429 F. 3d 769 (5th Cir. 1982); *Matthews v. Kensington,* 12 F. 3d 399 (D. Haw. 1993).
- **Compare [case 1] with [case 2].** These signal words should be used when you are comparing the rules in two or more cases.
  - *Compare Gonzalez v. Smith and Co.,* 225 Vt. 456 (1982) (nominal damages of five dollars, claim dismissed), *with Jericho v. Collins,* 789 Vt. 156 (1979) (damages of $60,000, claim not dismissed).
- **But see.** When you are introducing an authority that contradicts the previously cited authority, you should indicate this contradiction by using the words *but see.*

  - Several states have maintained the traditional view of marriage as being between a man and a woman. *But see Peters v. Maine*, 589 F. 3d 695 (Me. Super. 1998).
- **Accord.** The word *"accord"* is used when one authority states your position exactly, followed by two or more authorities that support your stance but do not state it exactly.
  - *Johnson; Accord Rogers, Smith.*

SUMMATION

As you write, remember to always indicate where your information came from. Readers need to know that your arguments are based on trustworthy sources. A diligent tracking of sources is also indispensable in case you need to recheck facts or other information at a later time. Keep in mind that this chapter provides only a general introduction to a detailed and complex topic. To develop the skill of producing effective legal citations, it is best to familiarize yourself in depth with *ALWD* and/or *Bluebook.*

Chapter 15

Writing in the Criminal Case

WRITING IN THE CRIMINAL CASE is a form of advocacy. All stages of a criminal trial—pretrial to post-trial—require advocacy. The United States Constitution protects the rights of its citizens, ensuring them a fair trial and proper representation. The role of a lawyer is to represent and advocate on behalf of another person. In addition to oral argument, writing plays a major role in this advocacy.

IN THIS CHAPTER	

• **Adversarial Nature**
• **Pretrial Writing**
  ○ Charging Documents and Indictments
  ○ Pretrial Motions
	• **Appellate Briefs**
	  ○ Types of Appeals
	  ○ Appeals Process
	• **Summation**

ADVERSARIAL NATURE

Advocacy is central to much legal writing. The forms of legal writing discussed in this chapter are used in advocating for a client when a contested matter exists. A contested matter is present any time two or more parties have conflicting interests. In these cases, the lawyer often must communicate with multiple parties—his or her client, the client's opponent, a third-party decisionmaker (such as a court or arbitrator), and supervisors and colleagues at his or her law office. Some of this writing will be objective. Objectivity is necessary when one is giving legal advice to colleagues and clients. Often, however, the goal of complete objectivity must be abandoned in order for the attorney to effectively serve as a client's advocate.

Writing in criminal cases, as well as in civil cases, should generally be adversarial, not objective, in nature. Adversarial legal writing is not the opposite of objective writing, but it is quite different. It takes a stance and advocates one side of an issue, developing arguments to support only the client's position. It is important to remember that adversarial writing should never engage in deception; facts and laws should never be obscured or presented in such a way that the message is confusing. Adversarial writing also does not mean that a writer avoids mentioning the negative aspects of a case. This type of writing still must maintain some degree of objectivity. However, the facts and laws are presented in ways that support the client's position—supporting facts are highlighted, conflicting facts are explained and justified, and laws are interpreted to support the client's case.

Lawyers are advocates and counselors, but they are also officers of the court. They have a responsibility to uphold the law and promote justice, while also promoting their client's interests. Lawyers must help their clients determine the best option, which is sometimes cooperation or concession and other times more aggressive action. Adversarial writing should balance these roles—attempting to achieve both honesty and advocacy. As previously mentioned, these basic principles apply to both criminal and civil cases, although writing is often less central in criminal litigation. Below are some tips for successful adversarial writing.

- **Fifteen-minute rule.** Clarity and conciseness have been running themes throughout this book, and they are especially important in adversarial writing. Judges are easily overwhelmed; they have more than enough cases to work on and more than enough material to read for each case. Most judges will not tolerate complex, cumbersome, and verbose briefs or memoranda. Writers should strive to establish their arguments for busy judges and other readers in 15 minutes or less. Below are strategies that can assist in meeting the 15-minute limit.

  - Put the strongest material at the beginning of the document. Present enough facts, laws, and arguments in the first half page to convince readers of your position.
  - Advocate your position using the statement of facts.
  - Use headings in the discussion or argument section that are meaningful and engaging, clearly laying out your argument and guiding readers through the text.
  - Be as clear and direct as possible in the discussion and argument sections.
  - Use the conclusion to request your relief. New arguments or points should never be introduced in the conclusion, and it is also generally unnecessary to restate arguments that have already been made.

- **Remember your audience.** Audience analysis is discussed in Chapter 10 and elsewhere in this book. Though this practice is always important, it is particularly important when you are writing to an unfamiliar judge. Rather than accepting the uncertainty associated with dealing with an unfamiliar judge, you should do some research to find out more about the judge who is your audience. Make phone calls to people who are familiar with the judge. Use online resources, such as Lexis and Westlaw, to locate and read everything the judge has written in relation to the laws that apply to your case. Find out as much as you can about the person you are writing to, and tailor your arguments accordingly.
- **Conceding.** Use discretion regarding the facts and arguments of a case. When it benefits your client, it is acceptable to concede certain facts and arguments. However, you should not concede anything if it will not benefit your client.

- **Know the facts.** Thoroughly familiarize yourself with your client's facts and the associated laws. Make sure your research and questioning are rigorous. If you know the facts and laws and can see the big picture, you can more easily recognize all available options. It takes time to do thorough research, determine the best options, and develop strategies, but these are necessary steps to becoming a successful lawyer.

PRETRIAL WRITING

Prior to a trial, you need to issue several documents to make a formal accusation and to determine the boundaries for the trial. Pretrial preparations may have a significant effect on the outcome of a criminal case.

Charging Documents and Indictments

The purpose of an indictment or other charging document is to present a formal accusation against a person who is alleged to have committed a criminal offense. It is then determined whether or not probable cause exists to make such a charge. This process, which serves to uphold Fifth Amendment rights of U.S. citizens, takes different forms in different jurisdictions. There are two general ways in which charging documents are handled. One way involves the creation of a grand jury.

- When a grand jury is used, the jury will hear evidence from the state. If the defendant wishes to present evidence to the grand jury, he or she may be allowed to do so. After hearing the evidence, the grand jury determines whether or not probable cause exists to believe that a crime has been committed and, consequently, whether or not to issue an indictment.
- When no grand jury is used, a charging document is filed directly with the court. These charging documents have a variety of names, including bill of information, accusation, and complaint. These documents both initiate criminal procedures and provide notice to the defendant.

After a charging document is filed, the judge holds a preliminary hearing to determine if probable cause exists.

If the grand jury or judge finds probable cause, the defendant can be held for trial. Regardless of whether an indictment is issued to a grand jury or another form of charging document is filed directly with the court, the content of these documents is the same.

- Charging documents clearly state the prosecution's allegations against one or more criminal defendants.
- Each allegation is listed as a separate count. Charging documents may list one or more counts.
- Each count should state the time, place, and manner in which the suspect allegedly performed the offense.
- Each count should be clear and concise, using simple and plain language.

In complex cases with many accusations, charging documents can be hundreds of pages long. Many charging documents, however, consist of only one page. The goal is to briefly state allegations in a straightforward manner, not to give all related details.

Pretrial Motions

The pretrial period is the block of time after the preliminary hearing, but before the case actually goes to trial. During this time, defenses are raised, facts are investigated, and formal requests of the court (called motions) are made. Both the prosecution and the defense generally appear before a criminal court judge to make pretrial motions, and these motions set the boundaries for the trial (if a trial occurs).

Many different types of motions can be made, analogous to pretrial motions in civil cases. Attorneys may file pretrial motions to request a time extension, to request that an opponent's case be dismissed or thrown out of court, to exclude certain evidence for legal reasons (such as privilege or undue prejudice), and to determine who must testify as a witness and who cannot testify. For instance, the prosecution may make a motion that the defense's primary witness—an elderly man with Alzheimer's disease—is not legally competent and should not be allowed to testify in court. Three specific types of motions can be made by defense attorneys:

- **Motion to dismiss.** A motion may be made by the defense to dismiss one or more claims that have been brought against the defendant. If all claims are dismissed, the prosecution can then appeal the case's dismissal or start over with a new claim. If only a portion of the claims are dismissed (two of five, for example), the litigation continues with the remaining claims.
- **Motion to suppress evidence.** Motions to suppress evidence claim that evidence used by the state was obtained illegally. When defense attorneys file motions of this kind, a burden is placed on the state to prove that there was no violation of the defendant's constitutional rights. If the state cannot properly defend the acquisition of the evidence in question, then that evidence cannot be used in court. The state will not be allowed to present such evidence as a part of its case and will have to proceed as if the evidence never existed. When a motion to suppress is successful, the state's case is severely weakened, and sometimes the state will voluntarily dismiss charges. Motions of this type are among a defense attorney's most valuable tools.

    Countless legal reasons exist to suppress evidence, and these motions can be very complicated even for the most skilled lawyers. One of the best-known grounds for a motion to suppress evidence is a police officer's failure to read a suspect his or her Miranda rights before beginning questioning. Once an individual has been arrested, it is illegal to question that person before reading his or her rights. If an officer fails to read these rights to a suspect, any information given during the period of questioning can be suppressed in court. Similarly, evidence obtained via an unlawful search and seizure can often be suppressed.

Another issue that often comes up in motions to suppress evidence is suspect identification. It is possible for eyewitnesses to identify the wrong person. It may be argued that a witness was lying, biased, or just honestly mistaken. It may also be argued that the identification procedure (such as the police lineup) was suggestive and led to bias. Motions that challenge eyewitness identification are strongest when no other means of identification exist—no forensic evidence, no identifying statements from the accused or co-offenders, and no record of similar offenses that may provide evidence of a pattern.

- **Motion for bill of particulars.** In a criminal trial, defense attorneys can also make a motion to request a bill of particulars from the prosecuting attorney. A bill of particulars is a set of written statements that give more details about the claim or defense. Thus, this type of motion demands more details about the charge.

Typically, the motion itself is short and formal; it is accompanied by a separate, longer memorandum that gives the legal reasoning for the motion. These documents should take a forceful and assertive tone, while also being polite and unemotional. In pretrial motions, rules from controlling authorities will trump policy and fairness arguments. Therefore, written documents should first focus on controlling authorities. Following the filing of a pretrial motion, it is standard for the responding party to file a response memo in reply to the motion and for an oral argument to be held.

APPELLATE BRIEFS

In the appeals process, writing is of critical importance. Appellate briefs require the highest degree of advocacy in writing. When you are dealing with appeals, written briefs are generally more powerful than oral arguments. Additionally, when you file an appeal, statistically you face an uphill battle, which makes the production of a powerful appellate brief vital.

Keep in mind that appellate courts must look not only at the rights of the individual party presenting the appeal, but also at the larger picture of the effect an appeal could have on the body of law and on future cases in their jurisdiction. Advocates should be careful not to overlook these opposing tensions. An appellate brief will be most effective when the larger body of law is addressed, in addition to the rights of the individual. Also, quality carries more weight than quantity. Your chances of winning an appeal are much higher if you can point to one major, unquestionable error as opposed to many minor ones.

Types of Appeals

An appeal can be filed during the pretrial period of a criminal case or after the final judgment. Petitions can also be submitted for an extraordinary writ. Types of appeals and appellate writs are discussed below.

- **Interlocutory appeal.** Interlocutory appeals are made prior to the trial and appeal a pretrial ruling that would significantly affect the case. Interlocutory appeals put the trial on hold. This type of appeal is prohibited in most jurisdictions; parties are generally required to wait until the trial is over to file an appeal. However, judges and appeals courts sometimes make exceptions and will certify an interlocutory appeal by either the state or the defendant, pursuant to local rules.
- **Appeals after the final judgment.** Appeals made after the final judgment in a case are more common and are among the rights of the criminal defendant. An appeal must be filed in a timely manner, however. There is a certain time limit for appeals directly after the final judgment of a case is entered. Rules regarding this time period vary by jurisdiction, but late appeals will not be considered. It is important to know the rules for your particular jurisdiction.

  Appeals may be made for a variety of reasons. An appeal can be made by the state if a trial court decides to grant a motion to dismiss a case. However, the state cannot appeal a "not guilty" verdict; that verdict is final. If a "guilty" verdict is returned, on the other hand, the defendant can file an appeal. Appeals can also be filed regarding issues and claims that were thrown out early in the case.

Although appeals following the final judgment are more common than interlocutory appeals and are part of a litigant's rights, they are still not easily won. Thus, it is important to craft appeals carefully, challenging only the most important issues, and to present only the strongest reasoning for your arguments. Written appellate briefs must be concise and powerful.

- **Extraordinary writs.** Petitioning for a writ is another way to appeal a case, but these requests are very rarely granted. Writs are initiated by petitions filed in appellate or reviewing courts. Many types of writs exist; the writ of mandamus and the writ of prohibition are the two most commonly requested writs in civil practice, and the writ of habeas corpus is among the most publicized and familiar writs. These three types of writs are each explained briefly below.
    - **Writ of mandamus.** *Mandamus* literally means "we command." Writs of this type are directed at a judge who performed an improper action, failed to perform a required action, or in some way took away a party's rights in an impermissible fashion. A writ of mandamus is intended to remedy an abuse of judicial power. If the writ is granted, the judge in question must remedy the situation by restoring the rights of the afflicted party, undoing his or her unlawful act, or performing the required action. In some courts, mandamus has been replaced by injunction. Injunction refers to a court order that provides equitable remedy in a given situation.
    - **Writ of prohibition.** Writs of prohibition are very similar to writs of mandamus, and the two have even become blurred in many jurisdictions. Prohibition, however, is intended to prevent judges from overstepping their legal boundaries. Traditionally, writs of prohibition have been directed toward judges who had exceeded their jurisdiction or legal authority.

  - **Writ of habeas corpus.** The writ of habeas corpus allows a prisoner to seek relief from unlawful imprisonment. *Habeas corpus* is a Latin phrase that literally means "you have the body." Petitions for habeas corpus are typically argued as ex parte cases, in which a judge decides the case without requiring the presence of all parties involved in the controversy. The court process surrounding habeas corpus determines whether the detainee received due process, not whether he or she is guilty. The writ of habeas corpus is essentially a civil attack on a criminal case and relies heavily on the writing of briefs.
- A writ should be requested only when a judge's decision is thought to constitute a gross injustice. There is no specific time frame in which requests for writs must be made; they may be made "as needed." Since the granting of writs is unusual and extraordinary, a lawyer's writing must provide irrefutable justification for issuance of the writ. You must cite the clearest authority possible, using the guidelines below.
  - The strongest possible authority is a case from a higher appellate court or the highest court of your jurisdiction in which a writ was issued because a judge performed the exact same action as that which you are calling into question.
  - The second strongest authority is one from a higher appellate court or the highest court of your jurisdiction in which a writ was granted in a very similar situation.
  - The third strongest authority is an opinion that describes the particular conduct you are questioning as a reversible error.
  - When a lawyer is forced to rely on authorities outside his or her jurisdiction, chances of winning are greatly diminished. At the very least, four or five examples from other appellate courts are needed.

Appeals Process

When an interlocutory or regular appeal is made, the following briefs are typically allowed: appellant's brief, appellee's brief, and appellant's reply brief. The appellant brief assigns one or more reversible errors to the trial court. Examples of errors that may be assigned are listed below.

- Improper jury selection
- Improper jury instruction
- Improper evidentiary ruling
- Clearly erroneous factual finding
- Juror misconduct
- Unconstitutionality of underlying statute

The appellee is then allowed to draft a brief in response, and typically the appellant can draft a reply brief in turn. Writing appellate briefs in criminal cases is similar to writing appellate briefs in civil cases.

SUMMATION

The ability to produce effective adversarial writing is a necessary skill for legal professionals. As you construct pretrial motions, appellate briefs, memoranda, and other types of documents, strive to clearly and concisely articulate your arguments in a way that will convince readers to adopt your stance.

Chapter 16

Writing to Confirm Transactions

IMAGINE THAT AN ORAL AGREEMENT is made between a computer manufacturer and a chip manufacturer, establishing that the chip manufacturer will supply as many chips "as needed" at "market price" for the next five years. After one year, however, the chip manufacturer gets a better offer—to become Apple's exclusive supplier—and backs out of the original agreement in order to work with Apple. Of course, this leads to disputes between the original parties. In court, the chip manufacturer denies the existence of the original agreement, claiming that the company never agreed to supply chips for five years.

The promises made between the computer and chip manufacturers were simply part of an oral agreement. No written, signed documents existed to confirm the prior agreement, so it is one company's word against the other's. Proof becomes a tricky issue, and without proof, a prior agreement may not be upheld in court. In a court of law, written documentation is more meaningful than a person's word. Therefore, it is essential to clearly document all transactions.

PURPOSE OF CONTRACTUAL WRITING

We make oral contracts all the time. For example, when you purchase a drink at a local coffee shop, you are creating a contract by orally and informally agreeing to pay a designated amount for the coffee drink. Oral contracts are enforceable in court if one of the involved parties can prove that the contract actually exists. Obviously, however, oral contracts can be difficult to prove and often amount to one person's word against another's.

There are times when oral agreements are not honored at all. Statute of frauds laws require certain specific contracts to be in writing and signed by both parties in order to be enforceable by law. Statute of frauds laws differ from one jurisdiction to the next, but typically cover contracts that involve the sale or transfer of land, pacts that require one party to answer for the debt of another, agreements that are not to be completed within one year, and some contracts for the sale of goods under the Uniform Commercial Code.

Even when statute of frauds laws do not apply, it is generally a good idea to have a written contract. Written agreements are more formal than oral agreements and are more readily enforced in a court of law. Contractual writing constitutes evidence when parties enter an agreement, making promises to do or not do certain things. In essence, contractual writings become "the law between the parties," serving as legally enforceable documents unless contrary to law or to public policy. Lawyers commonly use contractual writing in the following instances:

- Putting a tentative oral agreement in writing
- Financial, banking, and securities transactions
- Real estate and business deals
- Settling a case or dispute

ELEMENTS OF A WRITTEN CONTRACT

The elements discussed in this section determine the enforceability of a legal contract.

Meeting of the Minds

Contractual writing represents a mutual assent or "meeting of the minds" between the involved parties. This means that all involved parties have come to a common understanding regarding a legal obligation, and this shared understanding is commemorated in a legal contract. Contracts are not enforceable in the case of an inherent misunderstanding, such as one party in a sales transaction understanding the term "mustang" to refer to a car and the other party understanding the same term to refer to a horse.

Offer and Acceptance

Quite simply, one party must make an offer and the other party must accept the offer in order for a contract to be valid. A counteroffer is generally seen as a rejection of the original offer, not an acceptance. It is through this offer-and-acceptance process that a meeting of the minds is achieved.

Mutual Consideration

Mutual consideration refers to the idea that parties involved in a contract must exchange something of value with one another. For example, in a real estate agreement, the buyer receives the applicable property and the seller receives money. Thus, an exchange has occurred. Even promising just a penny may constitute mutual consideration. For example, one party may promise to pay one cent in exchange for a car, and this constitutes a binding contract. Traditionally, mutual consideration has been a requirement for contract validity.

Some civil law systems are moving away from traditional conceptions of consideration, holding that an exchange of valuable rights is not necessary, and that a contract can be based upon only an exchange of promises. For instance, if one person offered to give her couch to another person, and that person accepted the offer without providing any sort of compensation in return, an agreement has been made and the person receiving the free couch is entitled to it. Modern contract law also recognizes alternative theories, such as promissory estoppel, which requires that a promise be upheld if one party has relied on the promise and acted on it to its detriment. Promissory estoppel can enforce promises even when no enforceable contract exists. For example, if a charity has relied upon charitable gift pledges and has taken action with these pledges in mind, it may be possible to require that the charitable promises be fulfilled.

Competent Parties

For a legal contract to be valid, each party involved must have the capacity to enter such a contract and be considered legally competent. People who may be considered incompetent are those who are impaired because of drug use, those who are mentally impaired, and minors (under the age of 18). It must be clear that all involved parties were competent to make an educated decision regarding the terms of the contract.

Performance or Delivery

The action required by a contract must be completed in order for that contract to be enforceable. For example, imagine that one person agreed to sell a piano to another person for $500. If the buyer had paid the $500, then he or she could enforce the contract to require the delivery of the piano. If the $500 had not been paid, however, the buyer could not enforce the contract unless it explicitly stated that the piano would be delivered before payment was made. Likewise, depending on the terms of the contract, the seller may not be able to enforce the contract until the piano is delivered.

Good Faith

Involved parties are expected to act in good faith. Essentially, this means that the parties to a contract should not deceive one another and should proceed with honesty.

Congruence with Public Policy

A contract cannot be legally enforced if it violates public policy. For instance, a contract involving the sale of illegal drugs is unenforceable because it is against the law to sell such drugs in the first place. Also, keep in mind that public policies change over time. These changes will affect the enforceability of a contract. For example, a contract may be written regarding the sale of a handgun. If handguns become illegal two months later, that contract will no longer be enforceable.

COMMON CONTRACT PROVISIONS

Boilerplate refers to legal provisions that generally appear at the end of a contract and are intended to protect parties to a contract from potential disputes. These provisions are often thought to be routine and are typically skimmed over or ignored. But boilerplate provisions are much more important than many people realize. If a contract dispute occurs and parties end up in court, those "standard" provisions may determine who wins and who loses.

Take, for instance, *Cagin v. McFarland Clinic, P.C.*, No. 05-3592 (8th Cir. 2006). In this employment agreement between a cardiologist and a medical clinic, a boilerplate clause determined the case's outcome. Strong evidence may have existed to prove that oral promises were made in addition to those promises represented in the contract. However, this evidence was disregarded because one of the contract provisions stated that the written contract represented the entirety of the agreement, superseding all prior negotiations, discussions, understandings, or preliminary agreements. The contract also required any modifications to be made in writing. Boilerplate provisions are not always given such power, but in negotiated, customized contracts such as that in the *Cagin* case, the boilerplate is capable of determining the case's outcome.

Thus, all parts of a contract, including the seemingly insignificant boilerplate provisions, should be written and reviewed with care. Several examples of common contract provisions are discussed below. Not all of these provisions will be needed in every contract. Relevant provisions should be included and should be modified to meet the needs of all parties.

Modification of Contract

As mentioned in the example above, provisions are often included that specify a process for making modifications or amendments to a contract. For example, it is common for a modification provision to state that all modifications must be made in writing and signed by both parties.

Notice

When a contract is being terminated, the terminating party is often required to give notice of the termination. The notice provision gives directions for how to send such notice, including the names and addresses of the persons to whom notice should be sent.

Assignment

Assignment refers to the transfer of one party's contractual rights and/or duties. The original party to the contract (known as the assignor) may find another party (known as the assignee) to take over his or her contractual obligations. If either original party wants to deal only with the other original party to the contract, and not with an assignee, then the contract should be written to explicitly prohibit assignment. If no assignment provision is included in the contract, then either party may assign or transfer the contract at any time.

Choice of Law

Choice-of-law clauses designate which state's law will apply if a contract dispute arises. Contracts are frequently made between two parties who live in different states, and it may be helpful for the contract to specify the law that will govern disputes.

Dispute Resolution

Provisions are sometimes included that specify dispute resolution procedures. These clauses can make dispute resolution more efficient and cost-effective. Dispute resolution clauses may provide alternatives or mandatory precursors to litigation, such as negotiation, mediation, expert determination, or arbitration. When no dispute resolution clause is present, then either party may begin court proceedings in the case of a dispute.

Cognovit Provision

Cognovit provisions require one party to agree to be judged in court without any notice and without opportunity to present a defense in the event that he or she defaults on any obligations or otherwise breaches the contract. These cognovit clauses are strictly governed in most states.

Attorneys' Fees

Provisions regarding attorneys' fees typically require the losing party in any subsequent dispute to pay the prevailing party's attorneys' fees and court costs. If a contract includes no attorneys' fees provision, then each party is responsible for paying its own attorneys' fees and court costs.

Indemnity

Indemnity clauses require that one party compensate the other for certain potential losses. Essentially, one or both parties agree to insure the other against loss. For instance, a contract provision may require a party to bear the costs of lost profits, delays, claims, or damages.

Saving Clause

The saving clause is also known as the severability clause. This provision ensures that even if part of a contract is deemed unenforceable, the entire contract will not be invalidated. The unenforceable portion of the contract will be discarded, but the valid portion will remain enforceable.

Non-Waiver Clause

If one party fails to comply with the contract terms, and this noncompliant behavior is excused by the other party for a period of time, the enforceability of the original contract may be lost. For instance, imagine that one party is required to make monthly payments to the other party but fails to do so, making only bimonthly payments for an entire year. If the bimonthly payments are accepted during that year, they may no longer constitute a breach of the contract. With a non-waiver clause, however, the original terms of the contract are generally enforceable despite any inconsistent behavior. Non-waiver clauses specify that one party will not waive the terms of the original contract through inattention.

Merger and Integration

As occurred in the *Cagin* case, a provision can be included that makes a contract an all-inclusive, final, and complete agreement. This provision holds that no other agreements are valid and prevents any one party from claiming that additional, extraneous agreements exist to nullify or modify a portion of the contract. Of course, in entering a contract with a merger-and-integration clause, it is beneficial for both parties to ensure that all promises and agreements are actually included in the written contract, as it may be impossible to enforce unwritten promises at a later time.

Counterparts Clause

A counterparts clause allows a contract to be signed in two different locations at two different times. If all parties get together in one place at one time to sign the contract, no counterparts clause is needed. But any time contracts are signed independently of one another, a counterparts clause should appear. It is important for each party to sign at least as many copies of the contract as there are parties and to distribute a signed copy of the contract to each involved party.

GENERAL PRINCIPLES OF CONTRACTUAL WRITING

Although contractual writings will vary in format, content, and language, there are a few general guidelines that should be followed.

Strive for Precision

Above all, it is necessary to be precise in legal writing that confirms transactions. Do not write in such a way that only your client can grasp the contract's meaning. The meaning of an agreement should be clear to an outsider who is not involved in any related oral negotiations or understandings. A person who is entirely unfamiliar with an agreement should be able to read a written contract and understand it completely—all terms, rights, obligations, and so on. Contracts should record with as much specificity as possible the rights and obligations of each party, as well as the time expectations for performance. The following guidelines can help you achieve precision in your writing.

- Clearly explain any details of the agreement that are potentially vague or ambiguous. If the agreement was drafted by an involved party, the court will often interpret any ambiguity in a way that works against the party who drafted the agreement. Define any terms that may be ambiguous to a potential reader. If you are using terms that have other commonly understood legal meanings, it is particularly important to define those terms.
- Precisely identify all persons, places, and things involved in the contract.

Follow Formal Requirements

Many documents have specific formal requirements that should be followed. These formalities may be drawn from statutes and regulations that have precise requirements and that define terms of art precisely. Examples include the Uniform Commercial Code, statutes on taxation, and statutes on securities. It may also be necessary to utilize precedential language. Court decisions become standards for similar cases that arise in the future. By incorporating the language that courts have already used, you can help ensure that your document will have the desired effect.

Tailor the Content

When you write a contract, it is always necessary to consider specific issues as they apply to the perspective of the party you represent. Here are a few examples of how you might tailor a contract to meet your client's needs.

- When determining remedy provisions, consider which party is more likely to breach. If your client is more likely to breach, then you may want to avoid including an attorneys' fees provision.

- When writing a multi-year contract on behalf of a supplier, you may want to consider the use of clauses that would excuse performance and clauses regarding an appropriate index for escalating a price term.
- In general, multi-year contracts require the anticipation of potential future events that might affect your client's ability or desire to fulfill the contract terms.
- If the opposing party or parties involved in the contract choose not to be represented by counsel, you should consider including a clause to address that issue.

Confirm Oral Conversations

Take care to record and confirm the details of all oral conversations. You should always keep notes on important conversations, recording the time, date, and content of each one. In the case of a later dispute, these detailed records will provide better evidence than a person's recollection of a conversation. Future writing should then refer to oral conversations by time and date.

Following an oral conversation, it is often a good idea to write a confirmation letter as well. When writing a confirmation letter, make it clear that your purpose is to confirm an oral conversation that has already occurred. Spell out the details of what was said or agreed to in that conversation, and request a response from the person you are writing to. This letter will constitute a written record and can prevent future misunderstandings or complications. Below are several guidelines for the style and tone that should be adopted in writing transaction or confirmation letters.

- Be polite. Always take your audience's reaction into consideration.
- Indicate appreciation for the effort and cooperation of others.
- In general, be concise and formal. A more personal tone is sometimes appropriate when preexisting arrangements exist, but use caution with the incorporation of a personal tone.
- Double-check the details in confirmation letters before sending them. It is a good idea to review notes from the

conversation as well as any other relevant paperwork. Obviously, it is important to reiterate and confirm the established facts or agreements.

- The details of an agreement or decision should be fully repeated in your transaction or confirmation letter. This will give the reader a chance to identify and respond to any misunderstandings.
- Highlight any clarifications or amendments you wish to make, and ask the reader for a response.
- Send the letter in a timely fashion. It should be sent within a few days of the occurrence of a conversation or the receipt of a letter, report, order, or other document.

SUMMATION

Never lose sight of the importance of confirming transactions and producing written documentation for an agreement of any kind. If disagreements or problems arise later, written documentation will certainly prove useful. Without such documentation, an argument boils down to the word of one person against that of another, and prior arrangements may be difficult, if not impossible, to prove.

Chapter 17

Avoiding Common Mistakes

IN WRITING FOR THE LEGAL profession, as in any other area in life, mistakes happen. Although they may not be serious enough to threaten your life or career, they can lead to misunderstanding and cause you, the writer, to appear sloppy and unprofessional.

IN THIS CHAPTER

- **Spelling Errors**
  - Causes of Spelling Errors
  - Types of Spelling Errors
  - Remedies for Spelling Errors
- **Punctuation Errors**
  - Comma Usage
  - Latin Abbreviations
  - Apostrophes Denote Possessives, Not Plurals
  - Slashes
  - Ampersand
  - Ellipses
  - Adding Emphasis
- **Grammatical Errors**
  - Writing as If Speaking
  - Imprecise Word Choice
  - Vagueness
  - Pronoun Misusage

◦ Overusing Prepositional Phrases ◦ Overusing Quotations • **Errors Related to Legal Writing** ◦ Emotional Tone ◦ Burying the Lead	◦ Overcomplicating the Issues ◦ Mischaracterizing the Facts ◦ Making Projections • **Summation**

SPELLING ERRORS

Errors in spelling are quite common. A close look at restaurant menus, promotional brochures, or other literature will likely reveal at least one spelling error. Errors of this kind make the writer look unprofessional and careless. Carelessness in presenting one's message suggests carelessness in preparing the message. Thus, spelling errors can lead readers to question a writer's credibility and competence. You should be aware of common spelling mistakes in your own writing and take steps to avoid them.

Causes of Spelling Errors

The following habits can lead to errors in spelling as well as errors in grammar.

- **Sight-typing.** It is easy to overlook errors when you are watching the keyboard instead of the computer screen.
- **Unintended revisions.** Revision is an important part of writing, but it can lead to errors. Writers often edit their text but fail to inspect what remains after the edits. It is not uncommon for a writer to accidentally leave unwanted text on the page or accidentally delete desired text in the course of a revision. These mistakes can be easy to miss.
- **Mishearing/misremembering.** Some writers fail to use a dictionary or spell check to confirm their spelling.
- **Overreliance on spell check.** Other writers faithfully use spell check and trust that it will catch all possible spelling errors, which is often not the case. A spell check commonly misses "that" typed in place of "than," for instance.

Types of Spelling Errors

Some spelling errors occur because of omitted or jumbled letters. Sometimes a writer is thinking of the correct spelling, but his or her fingers skip over one or more letters. For example, a person may be thinking "purple" but type "puple" instead. A person may also think of the correct word but type the wrong word. Other times, a person's mind may jumble the letters of a given word. For example, a writer may jumble the *u* and the *s*, typing "sue" instead of "use." Spell check will catch some but not all of these errors.

Another common type of misspelling involves the use of homophones. Homophones are words that sound the same but mean different things and are generally spelled differently. There are hundreds of them in the English language. A few examples are given below.

- *Capital* vs. *capitol*
- *Tea* vs. *tee*
- *To* vs. *too* vs. *two*
- *Mourning* vs. *morning*
- *Which* vs. *witch*
- *Weather* vs. *whether*
- *Stationary* vs. *stationery*
- *Principal* vs. *principle*

In most cases, homophones will not be identified by spell check programs. If you write, "the state capitol is Springfield" instead of "the state capital is Springfield," spell check will likely miss the error. The word "capitol" is not a misspelling; it is just a misusage.

Remedies for Spelling Errors

The following suggestions may help you avoid misspellings and other types of grammatical errors.

- **Stay focused.** Watch the screen as you are typing, and don't allow yourself to be distracted by things like television or other media.
- **Be cautious.** If you are uncertain, take the extra time to verify your spelling and ensure that it is correct.

- **Be thorough.** Be sure to review your edits. When you have made revisions, it is important to read through the document to ensure that the text surrounding the revisions flows smoothly. What's more, take the time to read your document aloud and double check for errors. Spell check will not be able to interpret your meaning and catch errors such as homophones. After using spell check, it is important to proofread the document yourself.

PUNCTUATION ERRORS

As discussed in Chapter 12, it is important to follow the rules of punctuation to enhance the clarity of your message as well as your credibility. Punctuation should be used consistently throughout the entire document to ensure its cohesiveness and integrity. Some common errors in punctuation are discussed below.

Comma Usage

- **Which/that.** Different contexts are appropriate for "that" and "which." "That" should be used to identify a specific item or to narrow a category. It reveals essential information and is not preceded by a comma. "Which," on the other hand, is used to give additional information about an item that has already been identified. The information provided is nonessential, and therefore, clauses beginning with "which" should always be preceded by a comma.
    - Jim allegedly caused the injury that resulted in the plaintiff's hospitalization.
    - Jim's blow caused a skull fracture, which resulted in the plaintiff's hospitalization.
- **Who, where, when.** Similar to the rule governing "that" vs. "which," the use of a comma before "who," "where," or "when" indicates that nonrestricting, nonessential information follows, and the absence of a comma means that a limiting condition follows.
    - He was the man who left the scene of the accident at the corner of Broadway and Elm, where I live.

- **Such as/including.** A comma should not be used after the words "such as" or "including."
  - **Correct:** The witness remembered several details about the thief, such as her height and hair color.
  - **Incorrect:** The witness remembered several details about the thief, such as, her height and hair color.
- Also, observe the same rule regarding the restrictive/non-restrictive distinction represented by the comma as with "that"/"which":
  - I have listed all of the articles including references to that particular case.
  - I have finished reading all of the articles, including those with no bearing on this case.

Latin Abbreviations

It is best to avoid using the abbreviation "etc." It is generally ambiguous and unnecessary. If this abbreviation must be used, it should be preceded by a comma when it is the last item in a series. The same is true for phrases such as "and so forth."

The meanings of the Latin abbreviations "i.e." and "e.g." are often confused. The abbreviation "i.e." means "that is," whereas "e.g." means "for example." If either abbreviation is used, it should be followed by a comma. It is best in most circumstances, however, to avoid the Latin abbreviations and simply use their English equivalents.

Apostrophes Denote Possessives, Not Plurals

Keep in mind that apostrophes are used to form possessives, not to form plurals. An apostrophe is needed only if you intend to refer to an object or quality that someone or something possesses. To make a word plural, simply add an *s* with no apostrophe.

- The Smiths live here.
- Say your goodbyes.

Slashes

It is important to differentiate the forward slash (/) and the backslash (\). Writers are generally most familiar with the forward slash. This slash is commonly used to connect alternative options or paired opposites, such as "and/or" or "buy/sell/hold." The forward slash is also used in web addresses and to separate lines of poetry in running text. The backslash, on the other hand, is primarily used for technical matters, such as separating component folders, directories, or server spaces.

If a slash is needed, be sure that you are using the correct slash. For most purposes, a forward slash will be used. As discussed in Chapter 10, however, formal writing should avoid slash constructions like "and/or" altogether. Forward slashes tend to be overused and ambiguous. Attempt to say things more clearly and explicitly.

Ampersand

The ampersand (&) is used in place of the conjunction "and." It is generally inappropriate to use ampersands in professional writing. The only time an ampersand typically appears in legal writing is when it is part of an entity's title (such as a company name) or is used verbatim in some other context within a case. When an ampersand is used to connect two initials, no space should be left on either side of the ampersand (for example, Texas A&M).

Ellipses

An ellipsis is a group of three or four spaced dots (periods) that appear consecutively on the same line. When any part of a quoted passage has been left out—a word, phrase, line, paragraph, or more—this omission should be indicated using an ellipsis. When you omit material, take care to avoid misrepresentation.

Also be careful to use the correct form of ellipsis at the right time. A series of three dots should be used when the omission is within a quoted sentence. When the omission spans a sentence break or when one or more entire sentences have been omitted, a series of four dots should be used—the first one designating a true period (with no space before), which conveys the nature of the omission. Three ellipsis points may be preceded or followed by additional punctuation, such as a comma, colon, or question mark. Four ellipsis points (that is, a period plus an ellipsis), however, cannot be combined with other punctuation.

Ellipsis points are often not used before the first word of a quotation. However, if the quotation is started by a capitalized word (such as a proper name) that did not originally appear at the beginning of the sentence, the quotation should start with three ellipsis points. If the quotation omits the last part of the last sentence, four ellipsis points should be used.

- . . . Hamas looked outside of the Palestinian areas, to individuals, organizations, and foreign governments sympathetic to its mission, including the United States. . . . In 1987, the body within the United States–based Muslim Brotherhood primarily responsible for organizing the Palestinian efforts was the Palestinian Committee. . . . (*United States v. Holy Land Foundation,* CR No. 3:04-CR-240-G (U.S. Dist. Ct. Tex. 2007)).

Though appropriate for indicating an omission, an ellipsis should not be used to represent an incomplete or trailing thought. Rather than mystifying your reader with trailing thoughts, directly state what you are trying to say.

- **Correct:** We need to investigate this further.
- **Correct:** Do you think we should investigate this further?
- **Incorrect:** Perhaps we should investigate this further . . .

Adding Emphasis

- **Quotation marks or capital letters.** In formal writing, you should not put words in quotation marks or all capital letters ("the impact of the testimony was HUGE") to convey emphasis or flair. These uses for quotation marks and capital letters are inappropriate and unprofessional.
- **Italics, bold, and underlining.** Italics, boldface, and underlining can be used in moderation to impart emphasis or draw attention to particular words and phrases. These effects are overused, however, and should be kept to a minimum. It is also important to use these effects strategically so that the results are tasteful and consistent. Italics have specific functions—to identify titles of books and court cases, for example—but the other two effects are

primarily aesthetic. Italic or boldface words generally best convey added emphasis; underlining is used less often. More elaborate effects (such as shadowing or three-dimensionality) should be avoided altogether.

GRAMMATICAL ERRORS

Grammatical errors can lead to much confusion in readers. Chapter 11 discussed the parts of speech and gave a few rules for their use. This section expands on the ideas from Chapter 11, noting common associated mistakes. Take care to avoid these mistakes so that you do not come off as careless.

Writing as If Speaking

Speaking and writing are two different means of communication that use distinctive versions of the same language. Speaking is more informal, allowing for false starts, repetition, hesitation, and corrections. Writing, on the other hand, is more formal, with an emphasis on correct spelling, punctuation, grammar, word choice, and structure. Writers usually do not have the chance to start over or make corrections; a written text is less malleable than spoken words. Many writers fail to recognize these important differences and end up writing the way they speak. Heed the following suggestions for distinguishing your writing from your speaking habits.

- Avoid slang and colloquial terms (such as "gonna" and "ain't"). These words are used in everyday speech and often make their way into writing. They are unprofessional, however.
- Avoid misused and paradoxical words and phrases, such as "irregardless" or "could care less." These phrases are improper variations of common expressions and have no place in either written or spoken material. Use "regardless" and "does not care" in their place.
- Avoid sentence fragments and clichés. Clichés are used too frequently (by definition) and often inappropriately, which can lead to serious misunderstandings.

For instance, one writer called the World Trade Center bombing "a comedy of errors."

Improper Word Choice

Often writers are not fully aware of the distinctions between words and end up using them (especially prepositions) incorrectly. Examples of commonly confused words are presented below.

- **"That" (essential) vs. "which" (nonessential).** As mentioned earlier in this chapter, "that" is used with phrases or clauses that add essential information to a sentence. "Which," on the other hand, is used to introduce information that is not essential to the meaning of the sentence.
  - Lack of clean water in Africa was the issue that (*not "which"*) upset him the most, and not the food shortage, which is a long-standing problem.
- **"Who" (humanizing) vs. "that"/"which" (dehumanizing).** "Who" introduces phrases or descriptions that refer to people; "that" and "which" introduce phrases or descriptions that refer to nonhuman entities or objects.
  - The man who (*not "that"*) just entered the courtroom is the primary suspect in the PETA case for killing a horse that had escaped from its stall.
- **"Although"/"whereas" (contrasting) vs. "while" (temporal).** Technically, "although" and "whereas" denote comparison or contrast. "While" is temporal, meaning that it introduces information that applies to a specific time and place and does not always hold true.
  - "Although (*not "while"*) I find this case to be petty, my client still has a chance at winning, whereas (*not "while"*) the last case I worked on seemed hopeless from the beginning," I remarked while reviewing the case with my supervisor.
- **"Because" (logically dependent) vs. "since" (temporal) or "as" (comparative).** "Because" is used to indicate cause-and-effect relationships; "since" and "as" should

be used to indicate temporality and comparison, respectively.

  - Because (*not "since" or "as"*) there had been a warrant out for his arrest since last winter, the defendant drove toward the Mexican border as fast as a NASCAR racer.

- **"Such as" (inclusive) vs. "like" (exclusive) vs. "as if" (comparative).** The phrase "such as" introduces a list that includes the item specified next. "Like" refers to a list of items similar to but not including the item specified next. "As if" denotes a comparative relationship.
  - People like (*similar to, but technically not including*) my mother-in-law, such as (*similar to and including*) Tami, Melissa, and Katie, are never happy with what they have and are always wanting something more, as if (*not "like"*) a new house or car would make them happy.

Vagueness

Certain word choices can make a sentence vague and ambiguous. Some problematic terms that inhibit clarity are discussed below.

- Dummy pronouns in actuality have no corresponding noun. This type of pronoun can be distracting and misleading, and it can add dead weight to a sentence. Sentences should be reworded to eliminate dummy pronouns. The dummy pronoun is underlined below.
  - **Clear and concise:** When conflict occurs between parents, children often feel responsible.
  - **Less clear and concise:** When there is conflict occurring between parents, children often feel responsible.
- Avoid using the word "with" as a conjunction. "With" is overused and can generally be replaced by a more specific word.
  - **Correct:** Everyone else fled from the room; only I was left to question the defendant.
  - **Incorrect:** Everyone else fled from the room with me being left to question the defendant.

- **Correct:** Having many creative ideas for advancement, she continually expands her small business.
- **Incorrect:** With many creative ideas for advancement, she continually expands her small business.

Pronoun Misusage

A variety of problems can arise from pronoun misusage. Make sure that you are using the pronoun in the correct sense and at the correct time.

- Don't confuse possessive pronouns with contractions.
  - *It's* (contraction for "it is") vs. *its* (possessive pronoun)
  - *They're* (contraction for "they are") vs. *their* (possessive pronoun) vs. *there* (pronoun used to indicate a place)
- Be sure to use subject pronouns to represent the subject of a sentence and object pronouns to represent the object of a sentence.
  - The following are subject pronouns: *I, he, she, we, they,* and *you.*
  - The following are object pronouns: *me, him, her, us, them,* and *you.*
  - **Example:** They (subject) will send the report to both her and me (objects).
- Make sure all pronouns agree in number with the nouns they represent: singular subjects need singular pronouns, and plural subjects need plural pronouns.
  - **Correct:** A lawyer will likely write many important documents during his or her lifetime.
  - **Incorrect:** A lawyer will likely write many important documents during their lifetime.

Overusing Prepositional Phrases

Prepositional phrases can be useful, but they should not be overused. Prepositions should be limited to approximately one for every ten to fifteen words. The use of prepositions can be eliminated by:

- Cutting a prepositional phrase when the context allows.
  - **Concise:** The most important person

- **Contains unnecessary prepositional phrase:** The most important person in this courtroom
- Cutting unnecessary prepositions. Often this can be done by changing a noun to a verb.
  - **Concise:** Our efforts to legalize marijuana failed.
  - **Contains unnecessary prepositions:** Our efforts toward legalization of marijuana failed.
- Replacing prepositions with adverbs.
  - **Concise:** The lawyer argued passionately.
  - **Contains unnecessary prepositions:** The lawyer argued with passion.
- Replacing prepositions with possessives.
  - **Concise:** The judge's generosity pleased me.
  - **Contains unnecessary prepositions:** I was pleased by the generosity of the judge.
- Using active voice.
  - **Concise:** The state of Nevada won the case.
  - **Contains unnecessary prepositions:** The case was won by the state of Nevada.

Overusing Quotations

Sometimes writers become nervous about wording things incorrectly, so they quote everything they possibly can, making their document a series of quotations. Particularly in the explanation and application sections of your writing, it is essential to provide your own analysis. You should provide the analysis in your own words and use quotations only to highlight the most important insights, explanations, or interpretations. Quotations are necessary to add credibility to your ideas, but they should be used judiciously. The text should be your words backed up by quotations, not quotations backed up by your words. (An exception may be the rule section of a document, where it is often necessary to quote heavily.)

ERRORS RELATED TO LEGAL WRITING

The following concerns are specific to legal writing and can be detrimental to the career of a legal professional.

Emotional Tone

Without question, law is a contest, and exchanges between opposing lawyers can get ugly and personal. This can lead a lawyer to adopt an emotional, personal, or heated tone. As discussed briefly in Chapter 10, however, it is best to conceal your emotion. This is true for all communication—both oral and written—but especially for writing since the written word lives forever. A letter, even if directed at an opponent, may be viewed by the court as an attachment to a brief. An uncivil tone in letters or briefs will offend the court and may also trouble your client.

One lawyer once wrote of his opposing counsel that anyone advancing such arguments needs psychiatric help. The court was offended and the lawyer who used the inappropriate tone ended up losing the case. Try to keep sight of your ultimate audience and goal. Do not get so caught up in making your opponent look bad that you forget about the legal issue you are arguing.

Burying the Lead

Often, lawyers make several arguments of varying strength in support of a single legal point. It is essential to lead with your best argument. Don't allow the strongest argument to become buried by weaker points. Follow this rule even when you are responding to your opponent's arguments. Your opponent should be expected to present arguments in the best order for his or her client. You should do the same rather than following your opponent's chosen order.

Overcomplicating the Issues

As briefly discussed in Chapter 8, good legal writing untangles complexities in a simple, comprehensible way. Essentially, a good advocate makes the complicated simple. Substandard legal writing loses effectiveness by making the simple complicated and, as a result, neglecting the most important points.

Mischaracterizing the Facts

It is tempting to mold the details so that they better suit the needs of your client. However, briefs are not written in a vacuum; the opposing side will have a chance to dissect your arguments. Glossing over or misrepresenting a detail that might hurt your case becomes a weapon the other side can use against you. Therefore, as discussed previously in Chapter 15, lawyers should not conceal facts or engage in deception. Instead, take the time to really ponder how to best address the weaknesses in your arguments. Pretending those weaknesses do not exist is not an option.

Similarly, mischaracterizing a case or pulling a quote out of context can be fatal. Even if your opposition misses it, the court and clerks likely will not. Further, if you win in the trial court based on a misrepresentation, the verdict is likely to be reversed on appeal.

Making Projections

Be cautious about making projections of the future in a client letter. A large part of practicing law is accepting that there are many things out of your control. A lawyer can influence, but he or she cannot control what a court or an opponent does. Thus, lawyers must be careful to avoid guaranteeing results. This can lead to unfair expectations and disappointment.

SUMMATION

Writing is a more difficult task than many people think. There are numerous things for a writer to take into consideration: spelling, punctuation, grammar, organization, style, voice, consistency, clarity, and so on. And that doesn't even account for the rules and conventions associated with a specific discipline. However, following the suggestions and guidelines provided throughout this book will help to make any kind of writing clear, credible, and respected.

Part III

Application

Chapter 18

Memoranda

AMONG THE DOCUMENTS YOU'LL NEED to prepare in your legal career are memoranda. There are several kinds of memoranda. This chapter describes the most common type of memorandum—a brief, informative document used to communicate within an office, such as between attorneys on the same side of a case.

IN THIS CHAPTER	
• **What Are Memoranda?** ○ Nature ○ Purpose • **Form** • **Style** • **Organizing a Memorandum** o Caption o Issues Presented	o Brief Answers o Statement of Facts o Discussion o Conclusion • **Summation**

WHAT ARE MEMORANDA?

Nature

The term "memorandum" obviously is related to memory, and memoranda are most often used as written reminders to supplement the memory. For instance, an attorney might send his or her supervisor a memorandum detailing pertinent case information. Memoranda can also be used to relay inter-office messages, such as informing office workers of correct procedures during a fire drill. This type of memorandum is categorized as *objective* writing and can also be referred to as an *internal memorandum.*

The term "memorandum" can also refer to a document circulated between an attorney and a court. In contrast to objective writing, these documents are categorized as *adversarial* writing, or *external memoranda.* This chapter deals primarily with memoranda as objective documents. For more information on adversarial memoranda, such as legal briefs, refer to Chapter 20.

Purpose

Inter-office memoranda are most often used to communicate brief messages related to legal issues. For example, your supervisor might want to know whether to take on a particular case or might need an answer to a specific legal question. After carrying out research and analysis, you respond with a memorandum containing a concise answer to the question. This memorandum provides your supervisor with the necessary information to decide whether to take the case or how to argue the legal problem.

Given that your memoranda will be circulated primarily within your office, unlike a client letter (see Chapter 23), expect your reader to have a background in law and to be familiar with legal language. However, be careful not to assume that your reader has any prior knowledge about the particular problem or case your memorandum addresses.

FORM

Memoranda are organized with the objective of conveying ideas as quickly and easily as possible to a potential reader. Generally, the most important information comes first, followed by levels of increasing detail and analysis. Although the format of a memorandum will vary from one office to the next, most memoranda will incorporate the following elements:

- **Caption.** The memorandum's heading, which provides basic information about the document—its writer, recipients, and subject matter.
- **Issues presented.** The questions the document is meant to answer.
- **Brief answers.** Short summary of the memorandum's conclusions.
- **Statement of facts.** Relevant, unbiased facts that support the memorandum's central claim.
- **Discussion.** A more thorough analysis of the facts and other pertinent details to support the document's conclusions.
- **Conclusion.** A reiteration of the document's central argument.

STYLE

Since memoranda are short documents intended to convey information quickly, the most important stylistic principle to observe is conciseness. Imagine you have a stack of documents on your desk and only fifteen minutes to read the entire pile. If you have only three minutes to spend reading a memorandum, you want it to get straight to the point. As a writer, keep your document organized so that a busy reader can get the most critical information first, followed by deeper analysis. Avoid superfluous details and peripheral facts. As discussed in Chapter 10, on style, eliminating unnecessary words not only shows consideration for your reader but also makes for more effective written communication.

Concentrate on the issue at hand. Rather than expound on a host of related theoretical points or historical background details, keep the information in a memorandum streamlined and tightly focused on the central questions.

ORGANIZING A MEMORANDUM

Caption

The caption tells the reader what she or he can expect from the memorandum by listing the people to whom the memorandum is directed, the individual who wrote it, and the most basic information about its contents. A caption should include the following information:

To: The recipient of the memorandum (for example, an attorney or the entire office)
From: The sender of the memorandum
Date:
Reference: Include case numbers or case names
Subject: The subject matter of the document, as briefly as possible

Issues Presented

For each topic addressed, the memorandum should lay out central questions to guide the discussion that follows. These questions should be brief and clear enough to give an overview of the memorandum's contents, but detailed enough to give the reader a clear picture of the specific answers it provides. They can be phrased either as questions or as hypothetical statements.

The issue presented should give an indication of all the considerations that are relevant to your discussion. Consider the following examples:

- **Overly brief:** Does an Illinois court have jurisdiction over Dr. Johnson?

(Neglects the circumstances under which an Illinois court should be granted or denied jurisdiction over Dr. Johnson.)

- **Clearer alternative:** Has Dr. Johnson established sufficient minimum contacts with the State of Illinois such that an Illinois court can exercise personal jurisdiction over him, when he never physically entered the State of Illinois but

> did treat an Illinois patient and prescribed medicine to him through communications over the Internet?

(Gives general information and touches on the specific issues at hand—Dr. Johnson's cyber-communication with the patient and his prescription of medicines to the patient.)

Brief Answers

Following your list of issues presented, provide a concise summary (two to three sentences) of your answers to the issues. Think of the brief answers as a concentrated summary of the discussion section that follows, giving your reader a clear sense of the memorandum's conclusions.

For instance, a brief answer for the previous example would identify a possible court ruling for Illinois's jurisdiction over Dr. Johnson, suggesting a course of action for your supervisor. Given the possibility that a memorandum may not be read fully, consider the brief answers one of the most important sections to keep clear, streamlined, and informative. If nothing else, you want your reader to come away from this section with a clear sense of the answers to the memorandum's questions.

Statement of Facts

The statement of facts is one to two paragraphs of factual information relevant to the case, question, or problem. It provides the background necessary for the reader to understand the subsequent details and analysis of the case. Although the statement of facts is brief, it should thoroughly outline all applicable facts, including dates, names, locations, and an impartial account of parties involved and actions taken.

In contrast to the discussion, the statement of facts should be unbiased and free of legal analysis. Avoid inserting your own opinion or legal conclusion in this section. Consider it instead the foundation of necessary information on which your discussion rests.

Discussion

The discussion section is the meat of the memorandum, containing the in-depth analysis and research to back up the conclusion summarized in the "brief answers" section. It builds on the central question and the facts to detail the reasoning behind your conclusions, providing a clear explanation for your answer to the legal question. Although the discussion is the longest section of the memorandum, keep in mind the principles of conciseness. The reader will most likely skim the discussion section, so it needs to be written as clearly and tightly as the others.

Although the discussion is based on analysis and reason, it is still objective, not adversarial, writing. Rather than arguing for your personal opinion on a case, the discussion section should use facts and reason to predict the likelihood of a court's ruling on a particular issue. It should answer the question: under applicable law and given precedent, what is the likely outcome of the case and why?

Organize the discussion by providing one section for each item listed in the "issues presented" section. For each major issue, consider the following organizational guidelines:

- **Legal conclusion.** Structure each section of your discussion as you have structured the memorandum as a whole. Begin with the overall argument to alert your reader of your conclusions.
- **Relevant legal rules.** Discuss any statutes, regulations, or cases that apply to the memorandum's issue. If you find discrepancies between statutes or the outcomes of cases, use the discussion to analyze and reconcile these differences. Can conflicting issues be distinguished from one another (for instance, does one case apply more closely to the memorandum's issue)? Does one legal authority have precedence over another (for instance, did one case go through a higher court)?
- **Application to the present case.** Apply your analysis of these relevant cases to the issue at hand to determine a possible court ruling. Be careful to avoid merely restating the statement of facts. Use the discussion to apply reason and analysis to determine the most likely legal outcome of the case.

Conclusion

Though not always necessary, a short conclusion offers a place for you to reiterate and clarify the memorandum's arguments. Taking care to eschew repetition, briefly restate your legal conclusions. If appropriate, recommend a course of action for the reader. For instance, "Dr. Johnson can bring a Motion to Dismiss for lack of personal jurisdiction without fear of sanctions, but that motion is unlikely to prevail."

SUMMATION

A memorandum is a powerful tool when used correctly. It can provide an abstract of an issue or a case in thirty seconds' worth of reading and can carry enough information to convey in that half minute a half day's worth of research. Memoranda provide a record of the issues dealt with in a case in a brief, easily managed form. If one of your colleagues joins you on your case or you find yourself having to revisit an issue after a period of weeks or months, your memoranda can bring you and any others up to speed quickly.

Chapter 19

Pleadings

PLEADINGS ARE LIKE THE OPENING moves of a chess game. Pleadings, a set of documents that present each party's initial arguments, help determine the agenda of a case and help each party improve its case against the other side by introducing the main claims of each side. They also streamline how a case proceeds, by establishing boundaries concerning the issues that will be discussed.

IN THIS CHAPTER	
• **What Are Pleadings?** o Nature o Notice Pleading o Service • **Complaint** • **Answer** o Formatting	• **Other Common Pleadings** o Counterclaim o Cross-Claim o Impleader • **Summation**

WHAT ARE PLEADINGS?

Nature

Pleadings are documents that each party files with the court at the beginning of a case. In pleadings, each side of the case states its initial position on the legal issues. Each side lays out its complaints or initial answers, following specific formal guidelines, and these documents help shape the course of the trial. Pleadings occur before discovery, the portion of the trial where each side can request access to documents relevant to the case.

Jurisdictions and courts determine the exact requirements for the form of pleadings; however, pleadings always follow particular guidelines and are written in a formal tone. Courts often require specific language, or *terms of art*, in pleadings. When you are drafting pleadings, remember to include both legal and factual allegations.

Pleadings are composed of a series of documents, including *complaints* and *answers*. Traditionally, pleadings also included demurrers, which are now relatively uncommon. Complaints are formal documents filed by plaintiffs. Answers are the defendant's response to the complaints, which also follow specific formal guidelines. There are several types of pleadings, including common law pleadings, code pleadings, and notice pleadings. This chapter primarily covers notice pleadings, but also briefly discusses other common types of pleadings.

Notice Pleading

Common law pleadings and code pleadings, which were largely used before notice pleadings, often involved complicated or overly technical rules. The notice pleading, the most common form of pleading today, was adopted under the Federal Rules of Civil Procedure (FRCP) in 1938 with the aim of simplifying the rules governing pleading. The FRCP sought to replace the strict rules of common law pleading and code pleading, as well as incorporating several improvements. Notice pleading has several purposes:

- **Informing each party of the claims against it.** This allows each party to strengthen its case before discovery. It can also help the weaker side improve its case.
- **Eliminating cases without merit.** If a case *on its face* fails to establish jurisdiction or to state a cause of action, the

case can be dismissed after the pleading without the need for further discovery. This streamlines the legal process by allowing a case to be dismissed on a party's motion without discovery.

- **Narrowing the range of issues involved in a case.** Pleadings determine the significant issues a case will cover, eliminating the litigation of issues not pleaded in the initial documents.
- **Allowing each side to plead particular facts.** Even before discovery, each side of the case is given the opportunity to plead specific facts about the case as it understands them and to direct the course of the trial. However, since discovery can bring new issues to light, pleadings can be amended, although sometimes with restrictions for the sake of expedience or fairness.

Service

Pleadings require service of process, which means that the documents must be delivered to the person or people being served. In addition to being filed in court, full copies of the pleadings must be delivered to the adverse party (or its attorney or representation). Each jurisdiction has particular rules governing service of process; however, complaints must generally be delivered in person and by someone not involved in the litigation. They can be delivered through a public office (sheriff, bailiff, or marshal) or through a private process server (such as a private investigator).

COMPLAINT

A complaint asserts the plaintiff's cause of action and is one of the documents included in a set of pleadings. It is an official document that justifies the plaintiff's right to take legal action and lays out the facts of the plaintiff's charge.

Generally, the formal requirements of a complaint are organized according to the following categories:

- **Caption.** As with the memorandum, the caption of the complaint follows a specific form dictated by the jurisdiction. It includes the names of each party and of the court.

- **Preamble.** The preamble identifies the plaintiff and the defendant—for instance, "Ms. Earnshaw wishes to file a formal complaint against Mr. Heathcliff for damages against a valuable oak tree in Ms. Earnshaw's garden, where Mr. Heathcliff intruded." In addition, it lays out the overall claim against the defendant.
- **Numbered paragraphs.** Each paragraph sets out one or more distinct, specific allegations against the defendant. These claims support the plaintiff's cause of action and lay out boundaries for the content of the case. Together, these paragraphs should indicate sufficient justification for the plaintiff's allegation against the defendant and should support the plaintiff's entitlement to relief.
- **Prayer for relief.** Based on the numbered allegations, the plaintiff's prayer for relief is a request to the courts for compensation by the defendant. The defendant might request financial compensation, damages, or injunction.

The complaint is a formal document justifying a plaintiff's claim against a defendant. Being the opening document in a case, a complaint should be written in a lucid, straightforward style. The defendant's answer will also be based on the information in the complaint; therefore, the complaint must be detailed and specific. A complaint can be dismissed; thus it is very important to include all relevant information.

ANSWER

The answer is the defendant's preliminary response to the plaintiff's complaint. It acknowledges receipt of the complaint and lays out the defendant's initial claims in response. Its response to the complaint shapes the progression of pretrial proceedings and of the trial. Thus, the answer, like the complaint, must follow particular formatting rules. The initial requirements for an answer are as follows:

- **Defendants.** The parties named in the plaintiff's complaint are the defendants, and they must file a response (or they may file a joint response).

- **Caption.** The caption of the answer must correspond to the caption on the plaintiff's complaint.
- **Time limit.** Defendants have a short period of time in which they must file their answer after receiving the complaint.
- **Dismissals.** Rather than respond to the complaint, the defendant has the option to seek dismissal of the plaintiff's claims. To do so, the defendant must have reasonable cause to move to dismiss the case (for instance, he or she may believe the pleadings do not state a cognizable cause of action). An objection to subject matter jurisdiction can never be waived. Personal jurisdiction, however, must be raised in the first filing. To move to dismiss the case, the defendant must file the motion with the courts *in place of* an answer. If the defendant files an answer and later moves to dismiss the case, the answer may result in the court's waiving the defendant's objection to personal jurisdiction.

Formatting

The formatting of the answer follows the formatting of the complaint. After the caption, the answer conforms to the following format:

- **Response to the plaintiff's allegations.** In paragraphs corresponding to the numbering of the plaintiff's complaint, the defendant lays out a response to each allegation. In the response, the defendant must admit to or deny each of the plaintiff's allegations. If the defendant is uncertain about the veracity of any of the plaintiff's claims, it is common to deny the allegation on the basis of lack of knowledge.
- **Affirmative defenses.** After replying to each of the plaintiff's allegations, the defendant lays out affirmative defenses. Even if the answer acknowledges all of the plaintiff's allegations, an affirmative defense makes a case for why the defendant should not be held liable. For instance, the defense might argue for statutory immunity or contributory negligence. Unlike a dismissal, an affirmative defense does not deny the validity of the plaintiff's claims; instead, it offers an explanation or argument for why the plaintiff should not be held liable.

OTHER COMMON PLEADINGS

The complaint and the answer are the central documents of notice pleading; however, there are other common pleadings included under the FRCP. Like complaints and answers, counterclaims, cross-claims, and impleaders are intended to streamline and clarify the terms of a case before it goes to trial. They facilitate the strengthening of the case on both sides and may narrow the issues of the case.

Counterclaim

Counterclaims are pleadings filed by the defendant in which the defendant makes its own allegation against the plaintiff. This establishes new causes of action while countering the plaintiff's claims against the defendant. For instance, a counterclaim might contend that it was the plaintiff, rather than the defendant, who caused an accident due to negligence.

There are two types of counterclaims: compulsory and permissive. A compulsory counterclaim is an alternative allegation within the same circumstances as in the original allegations. Generally, compulsory counterclaims are required to be filed in the defendant's answer to the plaintiff's original complaint. In contrast, a permissive counterclaim is an allegation unrelated to the circumstances of the original complaint. The court rules separately on the plaintiff's and the defendant's claims if they are not within the same case. A counterclaim must be filed with the defendant's answer in order to be considered. A compulsory counterclaim not filed during pleading may be deemed waived by the court.

Cross-Claim

A cross-claim is a document filed by one side of a case against a member of its own side. A plaintiff might make a claim against another plaintiff, or a defendant against another defendant. Cross-claims are similar to counterclaims in that they allow the defendant (or the plaintiff) to introduce an additional claim into the pleadings. For instance, suppose a school purchasing thirty computers sues the computer distributor and the shipping company for delivering damaged computers. The distributor can file a cross-claim against the shipping company (one defendant against another) in the same suit, requesting compensation for the damaged computers and denying its own responsibility for the damage.

The purpose of a cross-claim is to clarify the terms of a case and improve consistency by permitting the defendants and plaintiffs to make additional claims or nuance previous allegations.

Impleader

An impleader introduces a third party into a case. An impleader may be filed only by a defendant. The defendant makes a claim against a party who is neither a plaintiff nor a defendant in the original complaint (which distinguishes it from a cross-claim or a counterclaim). The defendant must argue that the impleaded party "is or may be liable" for plaintiff's claims against the defendant. The impleaded party is then served and incorporated into the case. For instance, if a patient sues a hospital for giving him contaminated blood, the hospital may file an impleader against the American Red Cross for supplying the hospital with the contaminated blood.

Impleaders streamline jurisdiction, improving efficiency in that two cases can be decided at once, as opposed to requiring two separate trials.

SUMMATION

Your pleadings set the course of your overall case. Although you are polishing your communication skills to present your case before the jury, you need them just as much in preparing your pleadings. Pleadings clearly set forth the merits of your case and can establish a position of power from which to advocate for your client throughout the course of the trial.

Chapter 20

Discovery

SOME OF THE OBJECTIVES OF pretrial procedures are to expedite the legal processes involved in a case, to reduce court times, to make trials more efficient, and to streamline the work of a jury or judge in determining the outcome of a case. Discovery, like pleading, occurs before a trial with the goal of clarifying or expediting a case. Discovery allows each side of the case to ask for and receive documents, evidence, and access to other information that might help them better understand the case and improve or otherwise modify their arguments. The process of discovery occurs after pleadings, but before trial. Ideally, discovery leads each party to understand both its case and its opponent's arguments more thoroughly. This greater understanding is intended to facilitate resolution by settlement or to set the stage for motions for summary judgment. In either case, the goal is to avoid trial if possible.

IN THIS CHAPTER	
• **What Is Discovery?** ◦ Nature ◦ Purpose • **Types of Discovery** ◦ Interrogatories ◦ Request for Production of Documents and Things	◦ Request for Admissions ◦ Depositions • **Writing Discovery Requests** • **Writing Answers** • **Summation**

WHAT IS DISCOVERY?

Nature

Discovery is a stage before a case goes to trial where both the plaintiff and the defendant can collect evidence relating to their respective sides of the case. Each party collects documents (or other evidence) either by request or through *subpoena.* Although parties to a case are subject to the various discovery procedures outlined below, third parties must be served with "process" in the form of subpoenas to compel them to provide documents, testimony, or other evidence. Discovery is aimed at controlling the number and nature of issues involved with a case by offering each side the opportunity to examine all the evidence before trial.

Each party is entitled to discovery of evidence that is relevant to the issues involved in the case. Such evidence includes that related to or relevant to a *material fact,* which is any document or other evidence that could shed light on one of the case's contested issues, or that could lead to further discovery. It is important to express discovery requests using language that is calculated to lead to the discovery of admissible evidence both directly and obliquely related to the request.

The process of discovery exempts certain documents, such as material that is legally privileged (for example, correspondence between an attorney and his or her client, or documents between attorneys detailing strategies for the case). Legally privileged information also includes certain protected documents between patients and their doctors.

A party may also refuse discovery, or modify the opposition's request, if the discovery is deemed burdensome, unnecessary, or overly burdensome.

Discovery is intended to clarify and support a case, not to inconvenience the opposing party. However, unilateral modifications of the opposing party's discovery requests are subject to challenge by that party and, ultimately, to review by the court.

Purpose

Discovery is important because it encourages parties to resolve claims before a trial (perhaps rendering a trial unnecessary). Most cases end in settlement after discovery, when both sides of the case have most of the information they would use at a trial. Settlements are easier on everyone involved, and they are less time-consuming and less expensive than going to trial.

Discovery may also facilitate alternative dispute resolution or a motion for summary judgment. Alternative dispute resolution, a type of settlement negotiated outside of a trial (and that may or may not involve third-party arbitration or mediation), can be more efficient than a trial. Both arbitration and mediation require a third party (sometimes a judge) to help reach a settlement. Both processes are voluntary, but in mediation a settlement or decision is not binding, whereas an arbitrator may impose a binding resolution.

Summary judgment is the resolution of a case by a judge or court, but without a full trial, which saves time and money for both sides of the case, and for the court. Both summary judgment and alternative dispute resolution expedite the resolution of a case and increase the efficiency of the legal system. Discovery can improve efficiency and catalyze these alternative processes.

TYPES OF DISCOVERY

Interrogatories

Interrogatories are inquiries that one party to a case serves to the other. The response to an interrogatory must be given under oath; thus, an interrogatory response functions like testimony in court. For instance, in a case where a moving company lost ten boxes belonging to the plaintiff, the defendant might draft an interrogatory asking the plaintiff about the contents of the lost boxes.

Request for Production of Documents and Things

A request for production of documents and things allows one party to request access to materials or other evidence relevant to the case that may be in the possession of another party. This procedure can also allow an opposing party access to inspect things such as a computer or land.

Request for Admission

A request for admission is an inquiry between the two sides of the case that demands a response to particular allegations. One party submits allegations, to which the other party must reply with a confirmation or denial. If the allegation is unclear or involves information unknown to the responding party, it is customary for the responding party to deny the allegation. This process may help narrow the issues involved in the case to facilitate further discovery, or to expedite the trial.

Depositions

Depositions are similar in form to interrogatories but involve oral, rather than written, testimony. Depositions are given under oath and in the presence of both parties' attorneys and a court reporter. Unlike a trial, they do not involve a judge. The testimony given during a deposition is legally binding and, like an interrogatory, functions similarly to testimony during trial.

WRITING DISCOVERY REQUESTS

The general format of a discovery request includes the following elements:

- **Caption.** Captions, also discussed in Chapter 19, include classifying information about the document. For a discovery request, this includes the title and number of the case and the court, as well as information about the party requesting discovery and for whom the request is intended.
- **Preamble.** In one to two formal paragraphs, the preamble gives notice that one party is propounding interrogatories, requesting production of documents and things, or requesting admissions from the other party.

- **Definitions.** Most discovery requests establish definitions of a variety of terms, including terms specific to the case and others, such as "document," that might otherwise be ambiguous.
- **Discovery request.** In the contents of a discovery request, one party specifies precisely what evidence or testimony it requires from the other party. A discovery request will also indicate which type of discovery one party requires from the other.
- **Certificate of service.** A written statement, signed and dated, accompanying each document filed and certifying to the judge that a copy has been provided to the opposing side.

Discovery requests are not the place to make arguments about the case; they are inquisitive documents and should generally be written in a neutral tone. Even though the goal is to gain access to the opposition's documents, parties should avoid making arguments about why they are entitled to the information. For instance, a discovery request should not raise claims that the other party is concealing important documents or evidence relevant to the case. In the case that the one party refuses the other access to documents or evidence, the court will later determine whether discovery is justified. It is not the responsibility of one party to intimidate or persuade the other into relinquishing documents or testimony in a discovery request.

In a discovery request, balance specific information with general claims. For example, if the plaintiff was involved in an accident where the defendant rear-ended his car, the plaintiff might request information about recent repairs to the defendant's vehicle. The plaintiff, on the other hand, might need information only about repairs to the brakes—but requesting more general information about repairs on the car might yield other information useful to the plaintiff's case. Although too broad a request—such as a request for all documents concerning the car—might lead to an objection, too specific a request risks the omission of pertinent information. Most requests are written broadly in order to elicit as much information as possible from the other side. If a discovery request is unreasonably broad, and thus intrusive and burdensome, a judge can later narrow the request.

WRITING ANSWERS

Like discovery requests, answers to requests should be written formally, concisely, and neutrally. An answer should concede or deny access to evidence depending on the type of request and the information requested. In response to requests for admissions, an answer should respond to each allegation individually, acknowledging or denying it. If a party is uncertain about the validity of a particular allegation, it is entitled to deny it for want of knowledge.

For interrogatories or requests for the production of documents and things, an answer should be written in the same way as a discovery request: succinctly, clearly, and neutrally. If the answer to a request is unknown, it is appropriate to indicate lack of knowledge, often by a denial. A request may also be objected to if the information is legally privileged. If the other party has requested legally protected information or otherwise made an objectionable request, avoid long-winded objections or arguments in response. Instead, briefly state your objection (for instance, the information is legally privileged) and let the court handle any questions the other party has about the merits of your objection.

If any issues arise with respect to discovery that cannot be resolved by negotiation, one party can file a motion to compel, which asks the court to adjudicate the validity of a refusal of (or other problem with) a discovery request. A motion to compel asks the court to require the party to hand over the evidence, documents, or information the other party believes it to be withholding.

SUMMATION

Discovery is a procedure that precedes the trial, with the objective of identifying and clarifying the evidence and documentation held by the opposing parties and thereby expediting, or possibly obviating, the trial process. Skillful planning and preparation of interrogatories, requests, and answers to requests can lead directly to a speedier and more efficient trial, or eliminate the need for one—either of which will result in significant savings in time and costs for your client and for the court system.

Chapter 21

Appellate Writing

THIS CHAPTER EXAMINES APPELLATE BRIEFS, written documents submitted to an appellate court during an appeal. In an appeal, each side submits briefs containing detailed arguments to support its position. These briefs are then reviewed by a panel of judges to determine the outcome of the appeal. You can think of briefs as written substitutes for a trial, but offering less opportunity for parlaying back and forth. As such, a brief must be clear and strong. Producing a strong brief requires strategy, research, clear writing, and ample revision.

If you have ever participated in a debate on a single issue or written a persuasive paper on a precise topic, then you already have some idea of what is required in a brief. A well-written brief presents a single argument and follows it—like a focused beam of light—to its logical end, while avoiding the areas outside the beam (digressions or points of less importance).

IN THIS CHAPTER	
• **What Is a Brief?** ◦ Briefs in Courts of Appeal (Appellate Briefs) • **Audience**	• **Form and Structure** • **Style and Tone** • **Summation**

WHAT IS A BRIEF?

A brief is a written document containing a sustained legal argument. Briefs analyze precedent and use evidence from the case to make arguments about why a lower court's resolution of a case should be sustained or overturned. Parties submit briefs—either during a trial, or to an appellate court—to persuade the court of a particular argument. Briefs submitted during trials are called *trial briefs*, and briefs submitted to appellate courts are called *appellate briefs*. This chapter will primarily cover appellate briefs. Occasionally, briefs go by different names, such as memoranda, according to court rules.

The goal of a brief is to persuade the court of your position using reasoning and analysis. Since they are persuasive documents, briefs use *adversarial*, rather than *objective*, writing. Unlike the tone of neutrality taken by an office memorandum or a client letter, a brief is successful when it influences a court to adopt your side's position on an issue.

Briefs in Courts of Appeal (Appellate Briefs)

Appeals are initiated by a party filing a notice of appeal. When an appeal is granted, a case moves to an appellate court, where the lower court's decision will be reviewed. The party requesting the appeal—called the appellant or the petitioner—files the first brief. The other party (the appellee) must file a brief in response to the appellant's brief within a specified period of time.

The appellant's brief argues that the trial court was in the wrong in some way and requests that its decision be overturned. The appellant may present myriad arguments about the inaccuracy of the trial court's decision, including:

- Incorrect legal holdings.
- Incorrect application of the rules of procedure or evidence.

- Problems or inequities involved with procedure, pretrial rulings, or conduct of trial.
- Clearly erroneous holdings of fact or factual findings underlying the lower court's decision. For the most part, appellate courts defer to the factual findings of the trial courts. Appellate courts reverse trial court factual findings only in the face of overwhelming evidence of inaccuracy.

Once the appellant has filed its brief, the appellee has a set period of time in which to file its brief in response. The appellee's brief should support the trial court's decision, arguing why it should be maintained and the appeal denied. Again, the appellant's response is in the form of adversarial writing, taking a position on an issue with the goal of persuading its audience. The appellee's brief is equally adversarial, addressing the contents of the appellant's brief and responding to each error alleged by the appellant.

Appellants are permitted to file a brief in response to the appellee's response, but are limited to existing issues and may raise separate points of error not included in the first brief. The appellant should respond only to the most important issues in the appellee's brief. For instance, an appellant's response should make an effort to counter any problematic or damaging arguments in the appellee's brief. The reply gives the appellant, who has the burden of proof, the last word.

AUDIENCE

The audience of appellate briefs consists primarily of appellate judges and their law clerks. Law clerks, typically attorneys early in their careers, are required to read and summarize a large number of briefs for appellate judges. Since law clerks are responsible for reading and evaluating the arguments of briefs, style and formatting are important persuasive tools. A clearly formatted, lucidly written brief will receive a different evaluation than one that is stylistically chaotic or difficult to follow.

FORM AND STRUCTURE

In matters of form, it is critical to adhere to the specific stylistic requirements determined by the court to which you submit your briefs. The first step to writing any appellate brief is a detailed review of the relevant court's rules of style and structure. There are, however, general structural guidelines to which most courts conform:

- **Title page.** Lists the important identifying information involved with the appeal.
- **Table of contents.** Notifies the reader of the contents of the brief and the location of particular arguments within the document. This, like the table of authorities, makes it easier for the law clerk to comprehend and process the material.
- **Table of authorities.** Lists legal authorities, statutes, and regulations to which the brief refers and the pages in the document in which they are cited.
- **Statement of the case.** Although the overall tone of the brief is persuasive, the statement of the case should remain relatively neutral, outlining the details of the case. The statement briefly recounts the facts of the case through its *procedural history*. The procedural history is a statement of the developments of the case in, and the decisions made by, the lower court. In some appellate courts' guidelines, the facts of the case and its procedural history will be separate. Occasionally, the statement of the case goes into more detail, citing specific events of the trial record that support the brief's overall conclusions. However, the statement of the case should maintain balance in its inclusion of detail. Disclose all significant details, but omit unnecessary or superfluous procedural facts.
- **Standard of review.** Set forth the standard of review for the appellate court to use to examine the decision of the lower court. The standard of review is occasionally incorporated into the argument section.
- **Summary of argument.** The summary of argument is an overview of your overall argument, one and a half to three pages in length. Because it is the first persuasive point in the brief and the first section your reader will encounter, keep the summary lucid, specific, and persuasive. Your reader will also use the summary of the

argument as a reference point for the argument itself, so it is critical that the summary be strong and complete. Typically, the summary of argument will be drafted after the argument portion itself is written, to ensure that all of the most important and compelling points are captured and that the argument is summarized as accurately as possible. Avoid unnecessary citations in the summary of argument. It is intended only as a brief outline of the argument to come; it is not necessary to flesh out the citations that the argument section will detail at length.

- **Argument.** The argument is the longest and the most critical section of a brief. Organize it according to the different issues you plan to address. Each issue should be preceded by a one-sentence heading that succinctly describes the main claim of the paragraph that follows. Think of these headings as summaries of the arguments for each individual claim. Following the heading is the content of the argument itself. Each argument should work toward synthesizing various authorities—the cases, regulations, and statutes—that guide the appeal. An argument should harness the principles governing these authorities to persuade the reader of the validity or illegitimacy of the decision under review.

  In contrast to trial courts, appellate courts are not bound to follow their own precedent. Thus, the arguments permitted in an appellate brief are not based solely on precedent. In fact, appellate briefs sometimes use authorities to persuade appellate courts to overturn prior rulings. Trial courts are bound by precedent and must follow appellate court rulings above them. Appellate courts, however, are free to revise former policies and to reconsider prior rulings. For instance, the Supreme Court is able to overrule precedent if the prior rulings are deemed unjust—a privilege lower trial courts do not share. The same privilege applies to appellate courts. Unless there is a controlling Supreme Court precedent, appellate courts are permitted to reverse previous rulings.

However, such reversals are unusual. The more convincingly you can claim that your arguments either fall within existing precedent or are a logical extension of such precedent, the more likely you are to prevail.

Since appeals can result in the overruling of trial courts, briefs may incorporate more analysis of policy and the intent of the law than many other legal documents can. Written documents for a trial court are less likely to discuss or challenge fundamental legal precepts, whereas appeals offer the possibility of deeper legal analysis and the freedom to discuss and challenge existing policy.

For each main claim in the argument section, consider using the following organizational structure:

- State the legal conclusion for which you are arguing, laying out your most important point first.
- Develop this point by evaluating the statutes, cases, regulations, and secondary authorities relevant to the issue. Use these authorities to establish a legal rule.
- Apply the legal rule to the present case to demonstrate the validity of your argument.
- Summarize or restate your overall conclusion.

- **Conclusion.** Use the conclusion of the brief to restate the relief your party seeks. For instance, you might request that a lower court's decision be overruled and judgment entered in your favor; you might request a new trial or affirmation of the lower court's decision. Avoid introducing new arguments, points of contention, or evidence for your case in the conclusion. The conclusion does not need to restate or summarize the main themes of the overall brief, since the argument section itself contains such summaries.
- **Appendices.** The inclusion of appendices is governed by local practices but, if permitted, appendices may be used as persuasive additions to your argument. You may include documents, exhibits, or testimony from a trial record, or you may choose to add evidence from particular authorities

to bolster your case. The contents of appendices are generally subject to specific rules of court.

STYLE AND TONE

Consider these few guidelines for developing the style and tone of a brief:

- **Avoid pathos.** Since a brief uses adversarial writing, it is not necessary to maintain the neutral tone you might use for internal memoranda, client letters, or discovery requests. Briefs are intended to persuade; however, certain modes of persuasion are more effective than others in legal documents. Avoid excessive emotionalism in a brief. Rather than drawing on pathos, or an appeal to the reader's sentiments, depend on logos, or logical progressions and careful reasoning, to persuade your reader.
- **Establish your ethos.** Adopting a tone of authority that gives the reader confidence in your conclusion is an important rhetorical tool. Use of an assertive tone will lend your writing greater credibility.
- **Transitions and flow.** Organize your paragraphs so that your reader can follow them easily, and take care to use transitions between paragraphs. Improving the flow of your writing is not only courteous to your reader, but also enhances persuasiveness. It is difficult to be persuaded by a piece of writing you can't follow.
- **Be concise.** Since briefs are long to begin with, it is especially important to keep your writing to-the-point and lucid. Omit needless phrases and words, and reread your document when you finish it to weed out any unnecessary language.
- **Avoid digressions.** If a topic, case, or example is not pertinent to your larger discussion or necessary to support your arguments, omit it. Again, with the lengthy nature of briefs, it is unnecessary to insert discussions or topics that are not directly relevant to your arguments.

- **Write clearly.** Communicate your meaning directly from the sentence level, through the paragraph level, all the way up to the document level. Pare down each sentence, leaving only the most important and clearest information. Keep your paragraphs tightly focused on a central issue, and focus your overall document on your central argument.
- **Check.** Review for grammatical, syntactical, and spelling errors, which erode your authority, distract your readers, and cast doubt on the validity of your primary argument.
- **Revise.** Revision is the single most important tool for writers. It enhances a piece's brevity, accuracy, and clarity and often helps you develop and strengthen your main argument.

SUMMATION

Briefs are the vehicles by which you draw the court's attention to the authorities and established lines of reasoning that form the foundation of your case. Writing a brief gives you the chance to set the direction of subsequent proceedings. Make use of the loosened requirements associated with the appellate setting to hone the arguments in your brief to achieve the maximum persuasive effect. As a result you will enjoy the privilege of the court's ear as you argue the merits of your own position and call into question the strength of your opponent's.

Chapter 22

Other Legal Writing

THIS CHAPTER ADDRESSES OTHER FILINGS you may encounter, focusing particularly on motions. In organization, style, and tone, motions are very similar to appellate briefs; however, they serve many different purposes. Motions are documents written by one party requesting relief—possibly even the termination of a case or trial. Depending on the point at which a motion is filed, different parties and different requests for relief are permitted. This chapter reviews the two most common types of motions: motions to dismiss and motions for summary judgment. It also examines general techniques for writing persuasive, lucid motions.

WHAT IS A MOTION?

A motion and its supporting papers are written to persuade the court to rule in your party's favor on a certain point or issue. The party filing a motion, called the movant, ordinarily files two documents: a motion and a supporting memorandum or brief. The motion is a formal document containing the specific request for relief (the types of relief requested depend on the issue at hand and can range from an extension of time or compulsion of discovery to monetary reimbursement or a new trial). The memorandum or brief is a supporting document detailing the legal and factual background purportedly justifying the court's granting the motion. The memorandum is longer and contains more detailed arguments to support the motion's summary request for relief.

In response to the movant's motion, the opposing counsel will file an opposition memorandum or brief responding to the movant's arguments and establish the validity of their own, competing arguments. The opposition brief will also draw on legal and factual background supporting the party's arguments.

COMMON TYPES OF MOTIONS

Motion to Dismiss

A motion to dismiss argues that a case should be dismissed entirely on legal grounds. For instance, one party might file a motion to dismiss on the ground that there is no jurisdiction or no cause of action under the law, based on the facts set forth in the complaint.

Motions to dismiss are typically filed and decided upon after pleadings are submitted, but before discovery is under way. Motions to dismiss are granted only if the plaintiff's claim is legally defective on the face of the pleadings. Without reference to any external evidence, the defendant must be able to prove the ground on which the case should be dismissed.

Motion for Summary Judgment

A motion for summary judgment seeks to prove that trial is not warranted. Unlike the motion to dismiss, a motion for summary judgment is generally filed after discovery is completed, and the movant can be either the plaintiff or the defendant. In order to prove that a trial is unwarranted, the movant must show both that there is no genuine dispute of material fact and that it is entitled to judgment as a matter of law, based on the undisputed, material facts.

When evaluating motions for summary judgment, courts view the facts of the case in preference to the nonmoving party.

DRAFTING SUPPORTING BRIEFS OR MEMORANDA

Motions and supporting papers follow style guidelines similar to those associated with appellate briefs (discussed in Chapter 21); however, supporting briefs and memoranda are generally shorter than appellate briefs. Because of this similarity in organization and style, it may be helpful to review Chapter 21 as you work on drafting motions.

While specific sections and overall organization will vary according to jurisdiction and the type of motion a party files, the following is a general outline of a motion's organization:

- **Introduction.** Begin with a brief preamble identifying the type of motion, the type of relief your party seeks, and why the motion should be granted. Follow with a paragraph or two briefly summarizing the basic argument of the motion.
- **Statement of facts.** Compile a summary of relevant facts that support the memorandum's central claim. This section should be a neutral record of the most important facts in the case.
- **Argument.** As with appellate briefs, the argument section is the core component of a motion. Lay out the central legal and factual basis supporting the motion—or, if you are the opposing party, the legal and factual arguments for denying the motion. Arguments for motions are similar in style, tone, and organization to the arguments in appellate briefs. Create a separate section for each individual element supporting the motion's overall argument. Each individual element should be preceded by a one-sentence summary heading, and followed by a

sentence or two summarizing the argument. Within each argument, work toward synthesizing various authorities—the cases, regulations, and statutes—that support the argument for a motion to dismiss or a motion for summary judgment. Each argument should aim at embodying the principles governing these authorities to persuade the court to grant or deny the relief requested.

  - For a memorandum in opposition to a motion, it is equally important to present your party's own affirmative arguments and to rebut the other party's arguments.

- **Conclusion.** Like the conclusion to an appellate brief, the conclusion of a motion is not a summary of the overall argument; rather, it is a request for the specific relief sought.

ORGANIZATION, STYLE, AND TONE

Consider the following stylistic recommendations as you draft a motion:

- **Explanatory synthesis.** The most persuasive motion is one that focuses on explanatory synthesis. In other words, it aims to produce a legal rule that supports the party's argument through unification of various authorities and cases. Motions use adversarial writing and need not be neutral. Writing a persuasive motion requires thoughtful analysis of legal and factual history, and connecting this history with the argument about the present case.
- **Anticipate opposing arguments.** When writing a motion, try to predict your opponent's arguments and preemptively disable their claims, if possible. Even on points where your opponent is likely to prevail, focus on the overall strength of your argument. For example, you might concede one argument to your opponent but point out that in light of various other arguments you have made, your opponent's single point does not justify granting your opponent's overall motion.

- **Choose controlling authorities.** Focus on rules drawn from controlling authorities. A persuasive presentation to the court relies on supporting precedent. For an issue to be reviewed, it must have already been presented to and decided by the trial court.
- **Use clear headings.** Organize the argument section around clear headings that make specific claims. This helps orient your reader and makes your arguments easier to digest, both qualities that increase the persuasiveness of your overall document.
- **Use citations.** It is useful to cite various authorities to bolster and emphasize your argument; however, make sure these citations do not disrupt the flow of your own writing. Try to incorporate citations into the flow of your prose. This has the effect of amplifying your persuasive power and giving the impression of controlling authorities seamlessly complementing and upholding your own claims.
- **Structure your headings.** Organize your headings around the rule you've derived from statutory or case law. For instance, if a motion is required to show three specific points to prevail, the three major headings should briefly indicate the contents of these arguments. Take care to distinguish between the different rules you establish through your authorities. In each rule's separate section, make sure to address any smaller issues. Leaving holes in your argument only provides an opportunity for the other party to undermine it and your motion. If there are any sub-elements or minor points, use sub-headings to address them.

SUMMATION

A motion is your chance to petition the court to rule in your favor. Its success depends heavily on the force of your arguments, bolstered by the facts of the case as they have been decided. A hastily prepared or otherwise flawed motion can accomplish precisely the opposite of its intended purpose. If you present a motion that assumes the truth of contested facts, its logic undermined by emotion, you are likely to meet with failure before the bench.

Chapter 23

Letters

LETTER WRITING IS THE BREAD and butter of any legal writer. In legal practice, letters serve a variety of purposes, and they are some of the most important documents an office sends and receives. Unlike memoranda, which are used primarily within the office, letters are used for communication with those outside the office. Letters are therefore more formal documents than memoranda.

This chapter reviews different types of letters you may be expected to write and lays out guidelines for organization, style, and tone. It also reviews the differences between office memoranda and client letters and gives suggestions on what to include (and what to omit) in client letters.

IN THIS CHAPTER	
• **Purpose of Letters** ◦ General Considerations for Letters ◦ Letter Structure ◦ Tone	• **Client Letters** ◦ Differences Between Client Letters and Office Memoranda • **Summation**

PURPOSE OF LETTERS

General Considerations for Letters

The most common recipients of letters are clients; attorneys or representatives of parties involved in your case, and third parties, such as health care providers or insurance adjusters. The goals of letters to such parties include imparting or requesting information, so both brevity and formality are necessary.

When writing a letter, you should ask yourself the following questions before you begin. Clarifying your aims before sitting down to write improves a letter's organization, tone, and overall communication.

- **Who is your audience?** Is your audience knowledgeable about the letter's subject matter? Is your audience interested in the content of the letter? Might your audience be hostile in any way? Knowing where your audience is coming from may be the single most important consideration in writing a letter, because it allows you to preemptively address any questions or doubts your reader may have.
- **Why are you writing?** Consider your ultimate aims in writing a letter. What is the letter intended to achieve? Do you want the recipient to respond with particular information? Do you mean only to impart a message? Are you trying to gain the loyalty of the recipient?
- **What message or content are you trying to communicate?** Are you trying to get access to the patient records of one of your clients? Are you trying to convey to your client what his next steps must be? Consider how much content

you want to impart to your reader, and keep your message free of digressions.

- **What style is appropriate, given your audience, purpose, and content?** If you are writing a letter to a client, your tone will be warmer than if you are writing to the opposite party's attorney. If you are writing to a third party, your message may have to be more succinct than one written to a fellow attorney in your own case. It is also important to consider how formal your writing should be.
- **What level of detail should be included?** Although letters should be concise and should omit any extraneous information, it is equally important to include all relevant information.

Letter Structure

Once you have considered these questions, it is time to map out the structure of your letter. Although the specific content of every letter will determine its organization, there are some important principles to follow and some general formatting guidelines for letters. A letter is structured in the following order:

- **Inside address.** This is the return address, the mailing address of the writer or firm.
- **Outside address.** This is the address to which the letter will be sent.
- **Date.** Include the day, month, and year.
- **Reference number.** Include a case caption or a brief indication of the letter's contents.
- **Salutation.** Generally, a formal salutation is appropriate, such as one beginning with "Dear" or "To."
- **Body.** This refers to the contents of the letter, whose specific organization is discussed in detail below.
- **Closing.** A formal closing, such as "Sincerely," "Best," "Yours truly," or "Respectfully," is appropriate.
- **Signature.** It is always necessary to sign a letter before sending it.

Within the body of the letter, there are several ways to organize your ideas. One acronym many letter writers keep in mind is AIDA, which stands for Attention, Interest, Desire, and Action. Observing these principles in this order will help keep a letter clear and effective. Also, be sure to limit each paragraph to one main idea.

- **Attention.** Open the body of your letter by grabbing your reader's attention and directing him or her clearly and professionally to your overall objective. If you want the recipient to send you files, say this in the first paragraph; if you want the recipient to simply sign and return a file, say so early on.
- **Interest.** Maintain your reader's interest by recognizing his or her needs. This may not be necessary for all letters, but it can be useful if you are writing to a third party who has been uncooperative and can make them more willing to help you, for instance. Say something like, "We are aware that we have already contacted you several times concerning these records, and we greatly appreciate your willingness to cooperate with us thus far and to provide this information."
- **Desire.** Create a desire in the reader to take the action that you want taken. For example, if you are writing to a client whose signature you need, you might point out that the sooner he or she returns the enclosed documents, the more quickly your legal team can return to working on the case.
- **Action.** What is your overall objective? Make sure you state your demand or need at the close of the letter, leaving your reader with the information he or she needs. Ask for the action you would like your reader to take, if any. It may also be useful to summarize any important information you have listed in the letter, to refresh the reader's memory.

Tone

Most letters you write will have a formal tone. The only exception to this formality requirement may be letters between two lawyers who are already familiar with one another. The chance to inadvertently offend is much greater through letters and e-mails than it is in face-to-face communication, so be sure to err on the side of formality if there is any question. The following guidelines may also be helpful in achieving the right tone for a letter:

- Be polite and deferential, but be careful not to allow your tone to become artificial or patronizing.
- Use clear language whenever possible. Do not sacrifice clarity for more important-sounding or more professional-sounding phrasing.
- Be concise.
- Be clear and firm in your position. Do not equivocate.

THE CLIENT LETTER

One of the most basic forms of correspondence is the client letter. Effective correspondence with clients is central to the success of a law firm, and knowing how to write a good client letter is important. Client letters often involve information about a case. After initial research into a problem or question for your client, you may need to report back to him or her about the likelihood of success on a particular issue. The research for a client letter is similar to that for an office memorandum, but the level of detail, the tone, and the organization of the overall document will be different. If, however, your client is also an attorney (for example, in-house counsel), a change in tone and structure may not be necessary.

When writing a client letter, consider the following recommendations:

- Avoid legal jargon as much as possible. Unless you know your client has legal training, such language may only alienate or confuse.
- If you do need to use legal jargon, be sure to define it in as clear and simple terms as possible. If your client does not understand the vocabulary of your letter, he or she will be unable to grasp its overall message.
- Give the client a clear and unequivocal conclusion concerning the legal problem your letter addresses. State this resolution early, and clearly, in the letter.

- Refer to legal authorities, but do so sparingly. Weighing down a letter with citations and references will only add to the confusion.
    - In client letters, there is no need for exhaustive treatment of the issue, or extensive citation of secondary authorities. Not only will a client often be unfamiliar with these authorities, but such nonessential details may alienate him or her.
    - Cite no more than one or two binding, controlling authorities and make sure you have clearly explained their relevance.
    - Avoid overwhelming your client with information; however, make sure the letter shows that you have done careful and thorough research into the problem. Leave the client with a sense of confidence in your research and your conclusion.

Differences Between Client Letters and Office Memoranda

Since client letters are communications between a firm and its clientele, they will obviously be written differently than interoffice memoranda. However, the content of these two types of documents will often be similar, since they both contain detailed answers to research questions. Here are some differences between the two that may clarify what to include, and how to structure, a client letter. Client letters to non-attorney clients:

- Are generally shorter. Because the audience is less familiar with the subject material, it is not necessary to include the level of detail you might in an interoffice communication. While an attorney might appreciate a greater level of detail to understand a legal conclusion, too many details in a client letter will only confuse a client.
- Are more formal and deferential. Since you are serving the client, it is important to maintain a formal and respectful tone in your correspondence.
- May need to explicate basic legal concepts. While you might assume that another lawyer will understand legal

terminology, client communications should stick to ordinary language as much as possible.

- Should be written with the client in mind. Write using the mindset of your reader, which will require empathy and sensitivity. Your client's life, business, or reputation may be invested in the result of your research. With this in mind, be careful not to give false hope to your client. If the news is bad, or your research yielded unfortunate results, say so unequivocally.

SUMMATION

As a lawyer, much of your writing will take the form of correspondence. Whether written to your colleagues or to your clients, your letters should be clear and specific, conveying essential information about strategies, methods, and proceedings. Remember that your letters should act as points of reference for their readers. Your intent should be unmistakable, your language transparent, and your tone professional. You may not always be available, but your correspondence is. Whether your letter presents questions or answers them, it should do so in language that is respectful and honest, acknowledging the investment that the recipient has made in the case.

Glossary

Active voice	Construction of an independent clause such that the subject performs the action
Actus reus	An action punishable under law
Adequate consideration	The return that a promisor receives for his or her promise, where all contracting parties receive each other's promises as consideration for their own
Adjective	A word ascribing an attribute to a noun, such as "hungry" or "tightfisted"
Administrative agency regulation	A law enacted by an agency created by federal law
Administrative rule	A judicial rule or regulation

Adverb	A word ascribing an attribute to a verb, such as "later" or "dreamily"
ALWD	The legal citation style used by the Association of Legal Writing Directors
Annotation	A collection of resources centering on a single topic
Answer	A defendant's response to a plaintiff's complaint
Apostrophe	A punctuation mark used to indicate omitted portions of words and to signify possession
Appellant	One who files an appeal
Appellee	An opponent to an appeal
Argument	A memorandum's claims, based upon the evidence surveyed in its statement of facts
Arraignment	The open reading of an indictment
Bail	Money placed in the care of the state to obtain a suspect's release from prison before and during trial
Balancing test	The weighing of multiple considerations against each other
Bench trial	A trial in which a presiding judge decides matters of fact as well as applying the rules of evidence and of law
Bluebook	The legal citation style most frequently used in the United States
Booking	Creation of an administrative record for an arrested suspect within a state's recordkeeping system
Borrowed rule	A rule borrowed from another case and modified to serve as the rule for a similar case
Bulleted list	A collection of related items displayed vertically, individually identified by bullets (dots or other simple elements) for emphasis

Caption	The heading of a memorandum, indicating its writer, recipients, and subject; or of a complaint, indicating the names of each party and of the court
Case location	The name of the reporter publishing the case
Case title	The last names of the individuals or the names of the organizations involved as the parties in a case
Certificate of service	A plaintiff or defendant's written, dated, and signed statement that discovery materials or court filings have been provided to all other parties
Charging document	A document clearly stating the prosecution's allegations against one or more criminal defendants
Circumstances	The sum of factors mitigating a criminal act despite the defendant's intention to commit it
Citation clause	A citation applicable only to a portion of a sentence
Citation sentence	A citation applicable to the entire sentence preceding it
Civil law	The branch of law that resolves disputes between individuals and organizations by providing redress; also, informally, law based on legislation
Civil procedure	The rules governing the practice of civil law
Closing argument	Evaluation of a trial before a jury by the prosecution or defense
Collateral appeal	A losing party's petition to a court of the first instance (a court of the same level as the sentencing court) that the presiding judge's final verdict not be allowed to stand
Colon	A punctuation mark used to introduce a subsequent item
Comma	A punctuation mark used to indicate a pause or division in the logical progression of thought
Commercial law	The part of civil law dealing with the enforcement of contracts

Common law	Law based on precedents created by court decisions
Complaint	A plaintiff's petition alleging a wrong and seeking legal redress
Complex-compound sentence	A sentence composed of multiple independent clauses and at least one dependent clause
Complex sentence	A sentence composed of one independent clause and at least one dependent clause
Compound sentence	A sentence composed of more than one independent clause
Compulsory counterclaim	A counterclaim that is factually related to the transactions and occurrences described in a plaintiff's complaint
Conclusion	A restatement of a thesis in light of qualifiers and rebuttals
Concurring opinion	Agreement with the majority opinion for reasons other than those held by the majority
Conjunction	A word connecting words, phrases, or clauses, such as "and" or "but"
Context	The assumptions made by the author or authors of a document
Contract	A legally binding agreement between parties
Corporate law	The part of civil law governing the creation and functions of corporations
Counterclaim	A defendant's complaint against a plaintiff, accompanying the defendant's answer to the plaintiff's complaint
Court and date	The court in which a case was decided and the date of its decision
Court of last resort	The most superior court in a given jurisdiction

Criminal law	The branch of law penalizing certain behaviors for the purpose of discouraging them in favor of other behaviors
Cross-claim	A plaintiff's complaint against a co-plaintiff or a defendant's complaint against a co-defendant
Cross-examination	Evaluation by the prosecution or defense of the other's evidence, including witnesses
Dash	A punctuation mark used alone or in pairs to set off a thought as an aside
Database number	A case's unique identifier, consisting of its year, the database in which it is recorded, and its document number within that database
Defendant	One against whom a plaintiff files a complaint
Deliberation	A jury's process of evaluation of disputed matters of fact
Demonstrative aid	A piece of evidence presented in court by other means than the testimony of a witness, whether as actual evidence (artifacts) or as illustrative evidence (visuals)
Dependent clause	A self-referentially incoherent grammatical element that contains a verb but lacks a subject
Deposition	The questioning of a witness under oath outside of a courtroom
Detailed outline	A stylistic outline expanded to develop each main point to the fullest extent possible by introducing levels of subpoints
Dicta	Judicial commentary and speculation regarding the case at hand, and thus not binding precedent
Digest	A collection of resources organized by topic
Direct appeal	A losing party's petition to a superior court that the presiding judge's final verdict not be permitted to stand

Direct examination	Presentation of evidence, including witnesses, by the prosecution or defense
Discovery	The stage of a lawsuit during which the parties collect facts; also called disclosure in the criminal context
Discovery request	A plaintiff or defendant's request to another party to produce a specified type or types of evidence, including through testimony
Dissenting opinion	Disagreement with the majority or plurality opinion
Docket number	The tracking number assigned to a case when it enters a court's schedule
Double quotation marks	A combination of two single quotation marks used in pairs to enclose direct quotations
En banc opinion	Agreement among a quorum (rather than a panel) of presiding judges
Executive branch	The division of government including a head of state and the ministers, other officials, and government workers in his or her employ who enforce the laws enacted by the legislature
Executive order	A directive made by a head of state or the executive of a region
Explanatory synthesis	A postulated rule underlying a memorandum's argument
External memorandum	A message relayed from a party to its counterpart and/or a court
Federal jurisdiction	The range of high crimes that national laws empower the national government to punish, such as treason and interstate crimes
Federal law	A law enacted by a national legislature
Felony	The most serious degree of crime

Fifteen-minute rule	A guideline when presenting an argument to do so in a quarter hour or less
Full citation	Complete reference to a case, including title, reporter, and court and date
Holding	The interpretation of a law in a particular case
Hyphen	A punctuation mark used to join words into compound words
Impleader	A defendant's complaint against a party not named in the case at hand who is or may be liable for the claim brought against the defendant
IMRAD	A mnemonic identifying the elements of good scientific writing: introduction, methods, results, (and) discussion
Independent clause	A self-referentially coherent grammatical element lacking a dependent clause
Indictment	The charge or charges against a defendant
Interjection	A word serving as an exclamation, such as "oh" or "well"
Interlocutory appeal	A plaintiff's or defendant's petition to the presiding judge appealing a pretrial ruling
Internal memorandum	A message privy to the prosecution, plaintiff, or the defense
International treaty	An agreement between nations
Interrogatory	One party's submission to the other party of a question requiring a response under oath
Judicial branch	The system of judges devoted to interpreting the laws enacted by the legislature in order to settle disputes
Judicial opinion	A judicial ruling

Jury instructions	Guidelines for reaching a legally admissible verdict, presented to a jury orally and in person by a presiding judge
Jury selection	The choosing of a panel of impartial citizens to judge matters of fact
Jury trial	A trial in which a jury judges matters of fact after a judge applies the rules of evidence and instructs the jury in the rules of law
Legal representation	A trained lawyer or team of lawyers
Legislative authority	The power to enact law
Legislative branch	The governmental unit comprising one or more representative deliberative assemblies that write and enact laws
Legislative intent	A legislature's purpose in enacting a law, as described in findings, reports, debates, and the like
List of elements	A range of characteristics whose presence or absence requires a certain decision
Local jurisdiction	The range of crimes, misdemeanors, infractions, and violations that local ordinances empower local governments to punish
Logical outline	A brief statement of thesis, qualifiers, and rebuttals
Majority opinion	Agreement among most of the judges presiding
Material fact	Evidence that relates to one of the contested issues of the case at hand
Mens rea	A defendant's state of mind while committing a crime (as purposeful, knowing, reckless, or negligent)
Minor	Someone younger than the legally defined age of majority, and thus treated differently under the law

Misdemeanor	The second most serious degree of crime
Misplaced modifier	The omission of the object of a dependent clause
Motion	A written petition to the court requesting that specific action be taken
Motion for a bill of particulars	A plaintiff's or defendant's petition to the presiding judge to require further explication of complaints or defenses from the other party
Motion for a new trial	A plaintiff or defendant's post-trial motion to the presiding judge that he or she order that a new trial be held, perhaps because of faulty procedure during the trial
Motion for judgment notwithstanding a verdict	A plaintiff or defendant's post-trial motion to the presiding judge asking that he or she overturn the jury's verdict
Motion for summary judgment	A plaintiff or defendant's pretrial motion to the presiding judge that he or she decide an aspect or all of a case based on the undisputed facts revealed during discovery
Motion to alter or amend a judgment	A plaintiff or defendant's post-trial motion to the presiding judge asking that he or she modify his or her judgment
Motion to dismiss	A defendant's pretrial motion, in lieu of an answer, asserting the lack of a legal basis sufficient to sustain a plaintiff's complaint
Motion to suppress evidence	A plaintiff's or defendant's petition to the presiding judge to disallow evidence obtained through illegal means
Noun	An entity, such as "sympathy" or "fruit"
Numbered list	A collection of related items displayed vertically, individually identified by number for easy reference
Opening statement	An argument presented to a jury by a party to begin a trial

Term	Definition
Oral advocacy	Verbal representation of a plaintiff or defendant expressed orally
Ordinance	A law enacted by a local body, such as a county or municipality
Parallelism	Presentation of related items in a consistent form
Parentheses	Two punctuation marks used together to set off a thought as an aside
Parol evidence rule	The inadmissibility in court of matters not delineated in a contract
Passive voice	Construction of an independent clause such that the object performs the action
Per curiam opinion	A collective opinion "by the court," even if not as a whole
Period	A punctuation mark used to indicate the close of a thought and to indicate truncation of words in some abbreviations
Permissive counterclaim	A counterclaim unrelated to the facts or occurrences of the complaint
Personal jurisdiction	The range of parties that a court can force to comply with its orders
Persuasive authority	That law and case law not directly applicable to the case at hand
Plain English	A method of communication preferring approachability in communication to exhaustiveness
Plain Language Movement	A school of thought opposing formidable wordiness among professionals
Plaintiff	One who files a complaint
Plea	A defendant's formal evaluation (usually of guilty, not guilty, or no contest) of his or her culpability pursuant to the state's charges

Pleading	Submission of a claim or defense
Plurality opinion	Agreement among the largest group of judges presiding when three or more opinions are held by the bench
Post-trial motion	A losing party's petition to the presiding judge that the jury's verdict not be allowed to stand
Prayer for relief	A plaintiff's petition to the presiding judge seeking redress
Preamble	A discovery request's description of its purpose
Precedent	The force of rules established by earlier cases
Preliminary hearing	A presiding judge's evaluation of whether or not the state can produce sufficient evidence to try a defendant
Preposition	A word explaining the relationship of one word to another, such as "to" or "over"
Pretrial argument	Less formal oral advocacy concerning pretrial motions and trial logistics
Pretrial motion	A plaintiff or defendant's petition to the presiding judge before a trial's beginning, often requesting the inclusion or exclusion of evidence
Primary authority	That law and case law directly applicable to the case at hand
Procedural history	The history of a case and its developments, including court decisions
Pronoun	A word standing in for a noun, such as "her" or "it"
Qualifier	An aspersion of part or all of a thesis
Question mark	A punctuation mark used to end a question
Rebuttal	An answer to a qualifier
Recognizance	A suspect or defendant's obligation to the state (e.g., to return for trial) pursuant to his or her provision of

	a defeasance (a promise or surety given in place of the obligation) such as bail
Record	The history of crimes previously committed by a defendant
Redirect	The final direct examination of a witness
Religious law	Law that relies on religious documents or a theological system as a source of reasoning
Request for admission	One party's submission to the other party of a factual statement, to which a response is required, thus establishing a fact for trial
Request for production	One party's request to the other party for a specific piece of physical evidence bearing on the case
Rest	The defense's or prosecution's conclusion of its case
Restatement	An authoritative statement of the law in a particular area
Review of bail	A presiding judge's determination of bail (or evaluation of bail, if already set)
Rule	A principle established by the interpretation of a law in a particular case
Secondary authority	Commentary on primary authorities
Semicolon	A punctuation mark used to separate independent clauses and to clarify complex lists
Sentence (grammar)	A self-referentially coherent grammatical element incorporating an actor (a subject) performing an action (a predicate)
Sentence (law)	The penalty inflicted upon a criminal
Serial comma	A comma used to separate the penultimate item of a list from the conjunction following it
Settlement	An agreement resolving a dispute between parties

Simple sentence	A sentence composed of one independent clause
Single quotation marks	A pair of punctuation marks used to enclose direct quotations embedded within other direct quotations
State jurisdiction	The range of crimes, misdemeanors, and infractions that state laws empower state governments to punish, such as capital crimes
State law	A law enacted by a state legislature
Statement of facts	A memorandum's summary of the evidence supporting its subsequent claims
Statute	A rule created by a body empowered with legislative authority
Statutory law	Body of laws created by the legislative and executive branches of government
Stylistic outline	A logical outline expanded to include an introduction and a conclusion
Subject matter jurisdiction	The breadth of matters that a court can adjudicate
Subject-verb agreement	Appearance in the singular form of a verb (action) performed by a single noun (subject), and appearance in the plural form of a verb performed by a plural noun
Subpoena	A court's order to a third party that evidence, whether artifacts or the testimony of a witness, be produced in discovery or brought before the bench
Substantive law	Law defining rights and duties, comprising statutory law and common law
Tense	A verb's designation of past, present, or future occurrence, as seen from the writer's viewpoint
Term of art	A piece of legal jargon often required by a court
Territorial jurisdiction	The geographical area throughout which a court exerts its influence

Text	A document
Thesis	A short, concise statement describing a document's purpose (and sometimes its content)
Transition	A word or phrase emphasizing the connection between two consecutive ideas
TREAT	A mnemonic identifying the elements of good legal writing: thesis, rule, explanation, application, thesis restated
Treatise	An academic resource dealing with the law
Trial	A public proceeding to evaluate the level of merit of the plaintiff's complaint
Trust	A legal instrument granting rights of property use to named parties other than the owner
Trustee	A party to whom a trust grants rights of property use
Unanimous opinion	Agreement among all of the judges presiding
Uncluttered page	A page format relying mainly on the arrangement of plain, simple text and white space to create the necessary visual emphasis
Unpublished case	A court decision not published in a reporter, whether because of its recentness or the level of its court
Verb	A word representing an action, such as "sneeze" or "sympathize"
Verb phrase	The combination of an auxiliary verb with a principal verb, such as "could happen" or "were jumping"
Verdict	A jury's final evaluation of disputed matters of fact
Voice (authorial)	An author's persona as conveyed by his or her writing style

White space	The area of a page occupied by neither words nor graphical elements
Will	A legal instrument granting rights of property possession to named parties other than its owner upon his or her death
Writ	A formal order issued by a court
Writ of habeas corpus	A court's order that a prisoner be released for reevaluation of the legitimacy of his or her sentence
Writ of mandamus	A superior court's order that an inferior court fulfill its duty expeditiously and in full
Writ of prohibition	A superior court's order prohibiting an inferior court from acting in excess of its jurisdiction

Index

About the Author

AMANDA MARTINSEK IS A CIVIL trial lawyer practicing with Cooper & Walinski LPA, where she is a shareholder, a member of the board of directors, and the Managing Attorney of Cooper & Walinski's Cleveland, Ohio, office. Founded in 1969, Cooper & Walinski specializes in advocacy and is the largest majority women–owned firm in the United States. Before joining Cooper & Walinski, Ms. Martinsek was a partner at Vorys, Sater, Seymour and Pease LLP, where she served as lead counsel in a variety of civil litigation cases. Prior to her work at Cooper & Walinski, she earned her BA in History, with honors, from Oberlin College in 1985. In 1991 Ms. Martinsek graduated magna cum laude from the New York University School of Law, where she was a member of the Order of the Coif.

Ms. Martinsek has been named an Inside Business Magazine Leading Lawyer every year since 2004 and was an Ohio Super Lawyer in 2007 and 2008. In addition to her professional accomplishments, Ms. Martinsek has actively served her community as a member of the board of trustees of the Murtis H. Taylor Multi-Service Center.